TABLE OF CONTENTS

Contents

THE SWING TRADER'S EDGE: FOUR STRATEGIES FOR TRADING SUCCESS

LEARN THE ART OF DECODING CHART LANGUAGE

DISCLAIMER

The information provided in this book is for educational and informational purposes only. It is not intended to be a recommendation to buy or sell any financial instrument or engage in any specific trading strategy.

Trading involves substantial risk and is not suitable for everyone. Past performance is not necessarily indicative of future results.

Readers are encouraged to consult with a qualified financial advisor or broker before making any investment decisions. The author and publisher disclaim any liability for any investment losses incurred by readers using the information provided in this book.

Ultimately, all investment decisions are the responsibility of the individual. The author does not guarantee the accuracy, completeness, or reliability of the information presented and shall not be held responsible for any errors or omissions.

ACKNOWLEDGEMENTS

I would like to express my sincere gratitude to TradingView(https://in.tradingview.com/) as all the charts which are used in this book are taken from it. This platform has been instrumental in illustrating key concepts and strategies, enhancing the learning experience for readers.

I am also deeply thankful to all those who supported me throughout the journey of writing this book. To my mentors, colleagues, and fellow traders who generously shared their wisdom and insights, thank you for your guidance and inspiration. Your expertise has been instrumental in shaping the ideas presented in these pages.

Lastly, I extend my heartfelt appreciation to my trading gurus whose teachings and experiences have profoundly influenced my approach to the markets. Your lessons have been invaluable in shaping my understanding of swing trading and navigating the complexities of financial markets. A special thanks to Peter Robbins and Frank Ochoa, they inspired me a lot and helped in shaping some of the ideas.

This book would not have been possible without the contributions and support of each and every one of you. Thank you for your unwavering encouragement and belief in this project."

INTRODUCTION

Welcome to the world of swing trading, where strategic analysis meets opportunity in the dynamic landscape of financial markets. In this book, we delve into the exciting realm of swing trading, offering you a comprehensive guide to mastering this art form.

Swing trading is a trading style that aims to capture short- to medium-term gains by identifying and capitalizing on market swings or price movements. Unlike day trading, which involves buying and selling within the same trading day, or long-term investing, which focuses on holding positions for extended periods, swing trading occupies a strategic middle ground.

Inside these pages, we've got four supercharged swing trading strategies just for you. Each strategy is carefully crafted to leverage market dynamics, technical indicators, and chart patterns, offering you a robust toolkit for success in swing trading.

Throughout this book, we will cover essential concepts such as trend analysis, support and resistance levels, monthly pivot strategies and risk management techniques. Whether you are a novice trader looking to build a solid foundation or an experienced investor seeking to refine your skills, there is something here for everyone.

Our journey begins by laying the groundwork for understanding swing trading, exploring the principles and methodologies that underpin this dynamic approach to the markets. From there, we will delve into each of the four strategies in detail, providing step-by-step instructions, real-world examples, and practical tips to help you implement them effectively.

By the time you reach the end of this book, you will have gained a deep understanding of swing trading principles and techniques, along with the confidence to apply them in your own trading endeavors. Whether your goal is to generate supplemental income, grow your investment portfolio, or achieve financial independence, mastering the art of swing trading can help you turn your aspirations into reality.

So, buckle up and get ready for a wild ride as we unlock the secrets of swing trading together. Let's make some waves and turn your financial dreams into reality!

PART-1
PRE-STRATEGY ESSENTIALS

CHAPTER 1

UNDERSTANDING THE 4 PHASES OF THE MARKET CYCLE

Just like the seasons change, the market moves through four distinct stages, each influencing how investors and traders make decisions. We'll take a closer look at these four stages in simple language, helping you understand the rhythm of the market and how to navigate it effectively.

ACCUMULATION PHASE: In this phase, smart investors quietly buy undervalued assets while prices are low. It's like getting bargains before everyone else catches on, similar to finding hidden treasures on the beach during low tide.

MARKUP PHASE: As more investors notice the bargains and start buying, prices begin to rise steadily. This phase is like riding a wave of optimism, where prices keep going up like a surfer riding a gentle swell.

DISTRIBUTION PHASE: When prices reach their peak, smart investors start selling to lock in their profits. At this point, others may still be buying in hopes of making more money. It's like the calm before a storm, where things seem quiet before a big change.

MARKDOWN PHASE: Eventually, the market turns, and prices start falling. Panic sets in as investors rush to sell their assets, often resulting in losses. It's like being caught in a strong current, struggling to stay afloat amidst the chaos.

Understanding these phases helps investors make better decisions, knowing when to buy, sell, or hold onto their investments. It's like knowing when to ride the wave and when to take a break on the shore, ensuring a smoother journey through the ups and downs of the market.

Understanding market structure isn't a walk in the park. It's like learning to swim – you can't just do it by watching online videos; you need lots of practice. But don't worry, it's definitely worth learning. Some market structures are easier to grasp than others, but the key is to practice by studying historical charts. Before diving into the upcoming chapters, it's crucial to be able to identify market structure.

Generally, there are four main market phases: accumulation, markup, distribution, and markdown. However, within a markup phase, you might notice some reaccumulation phases occurring before each markup phase. Similarly, you might see some redistribution phases before each markdown phase.

I'll provide examples of different types of market structure in the following pages to help you grasp these concepts better.

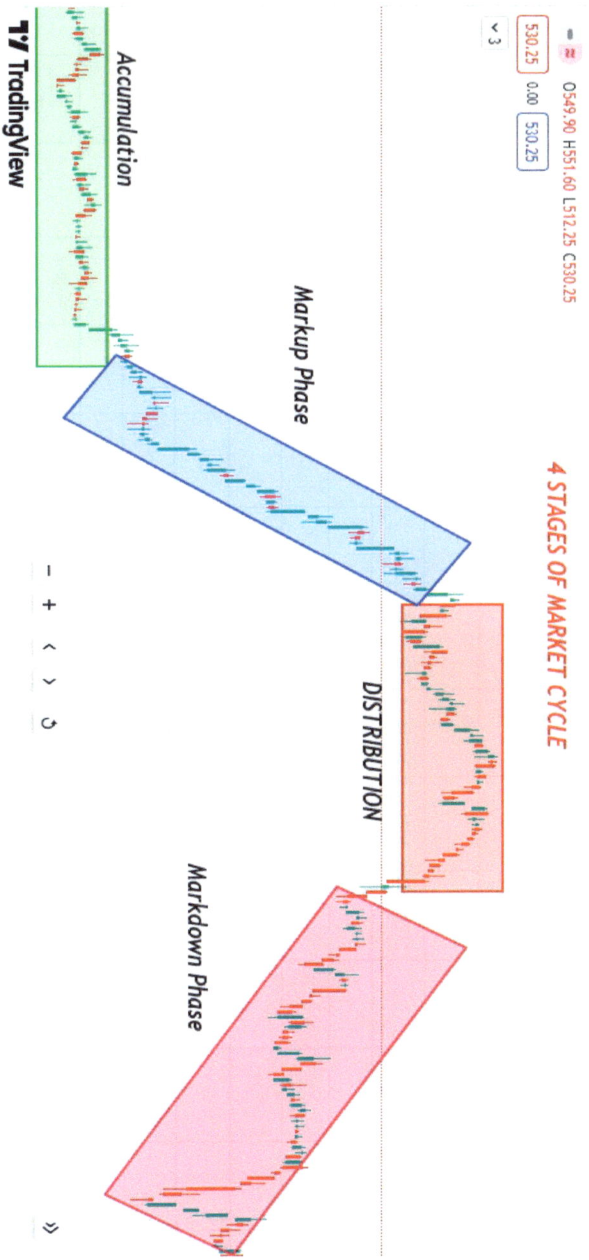
O549.90 H551.60 L512.25 C530.25
530.25
0.00
530.25
4 STAGES OF MARKET CYCLE
Accumulation
Markup Phase
DISTRIBUTION
Markdown Phase
TradingView

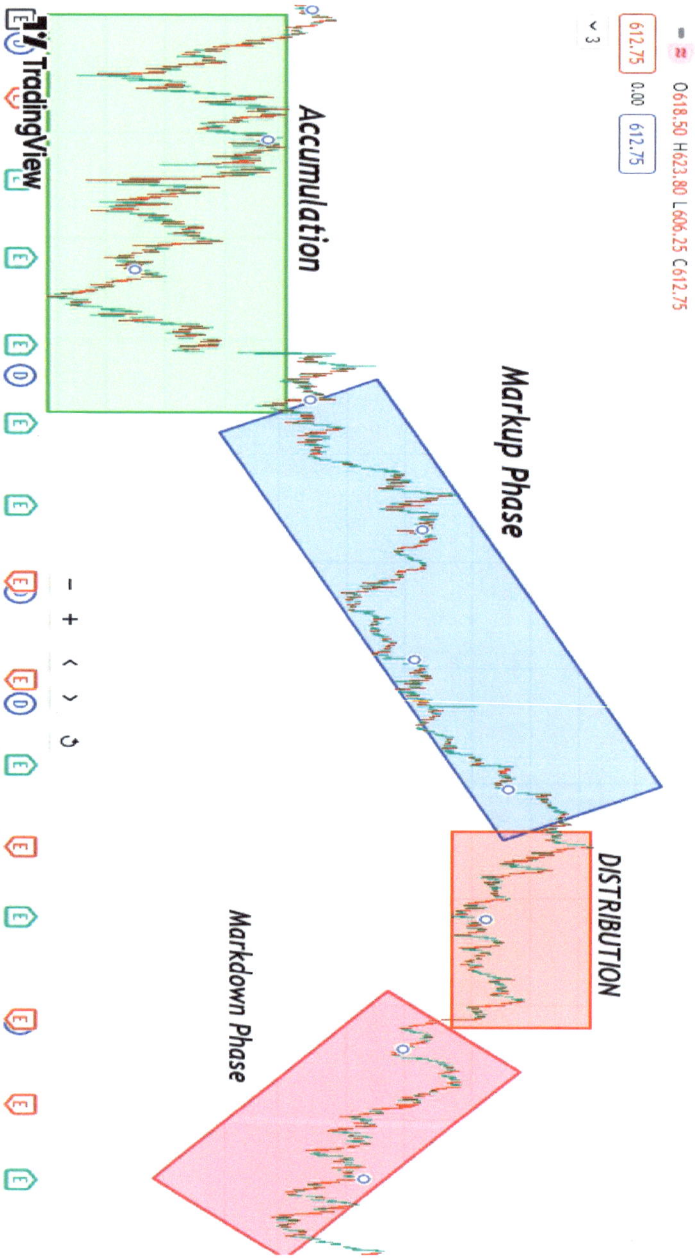
O618.50 H623.80 L606.25 C612.75
612.75
0.00
612.75
Accumulation
Markup Phase
DISTRIBUTION
Markdown Phase
TradingView

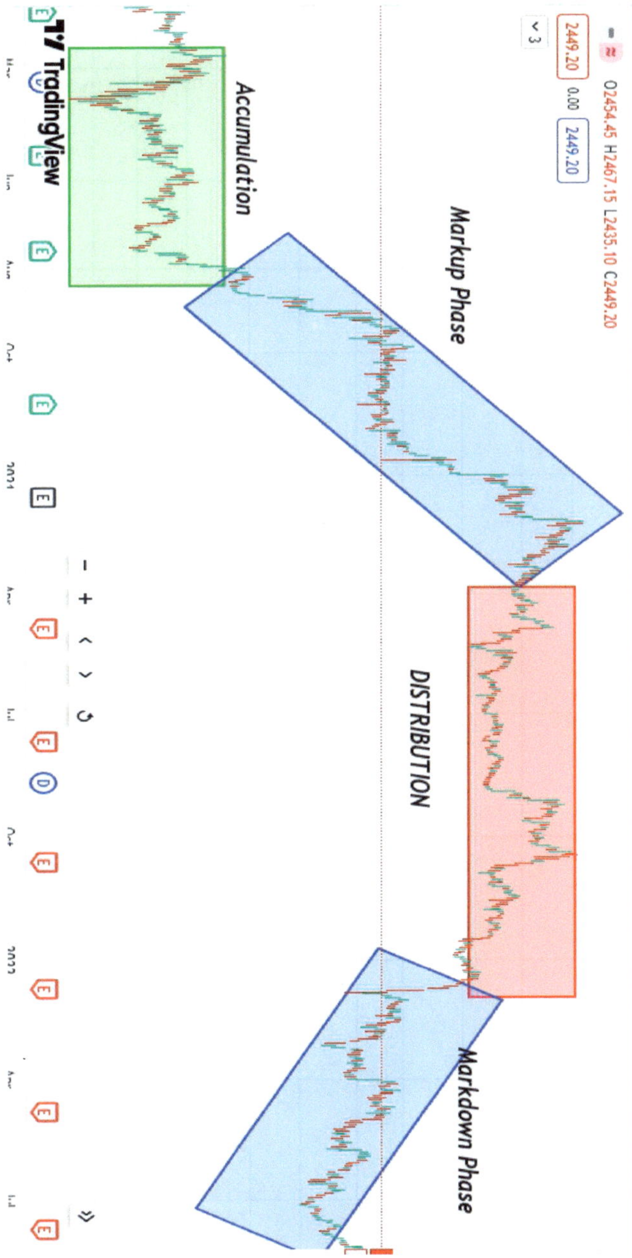
O2454.45 H2467.15 L2435.10 C2449.20
2449.20
0.00
2449.20
Accumulation
Markup Phase
DISTRIBUTION
Markdown Phase
TradingView

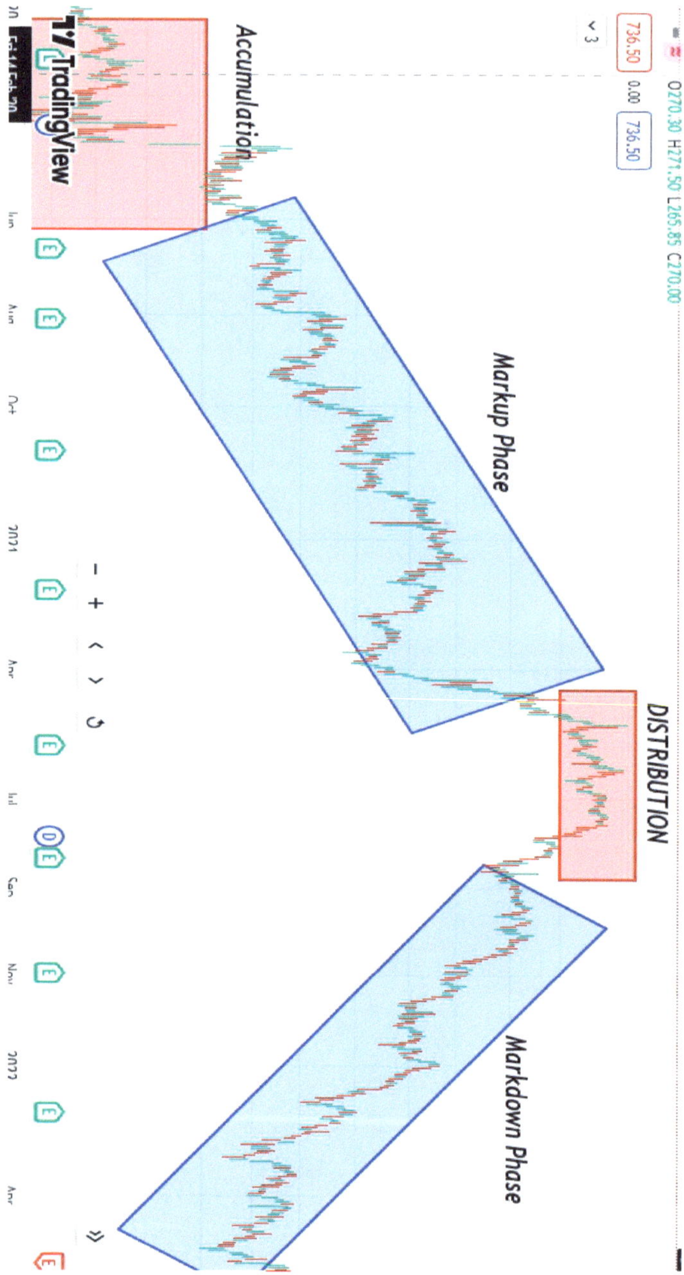
O270.30 H271.50 L265.85 C270.00
736.50
0.00
736.50
Accumulation
Markup Phase
DISTRIBUTION
Markdown Phase
TradingView

CHAPTER 2

CRAFTING EFFECTIVE TRENDLINES

WHAT IS A TRENDLINE?

A trendline is a line drawn on a price chart that connects two or more significant price points. It helps visualize the overall direction or trend of a market's price movement over time.

Importance of Trendlines:

Trendlines are important for several reasons:

Identifying Trends: Trendlines help traders identify whether a market is trending upwards, downwards, or moving sideways. This information is crucial for making informed trading decisions.

Support and Resistance: Trendlines act as dynamic levels of support and resistance. In an uptrend, the trendline often acts as a support level, while in a downtrend, it acts as a resistance level. These levels can help traders determine entry and exit points for their trades.

Confirmation of Trends: Trendlines can help confirm the strength and validity of a trend. The more times a trendline is touched or respected by price, the more significant it becomes, indicating a stronger trend.

Timing Entry and Exit Points: Trendlines can assist traders in timing their entry and exit points. For example, a break above a downtrend line could signal a potential reversal and a buying opportunity, while a break below an uptrend line could indicate a potential reversal and a selling opportunity.

Risk Management: Trendlines can also be used for risk management purposes. Traders can place stop-loss orders below an uptrend line in a long trade or above a downtrend line in a short trade to limit potential losses if the trend reverses.

In summary, trendlines are valuable tools for traders and investors as they provide insights into market trends, help identify support and resistance levels, confirm trend strength, and assist in timing entry and exit points. By understanding and using trendlines effectively, traders can improve their trading decisions and increase their chances of success in the financial markets.

Essential components for a effective trendline

- **Price points(highs/lows)**
- **Slope**
- **Reaction of price at trendline**

You should connect at least two peaks/highs to draw a valid trendline.

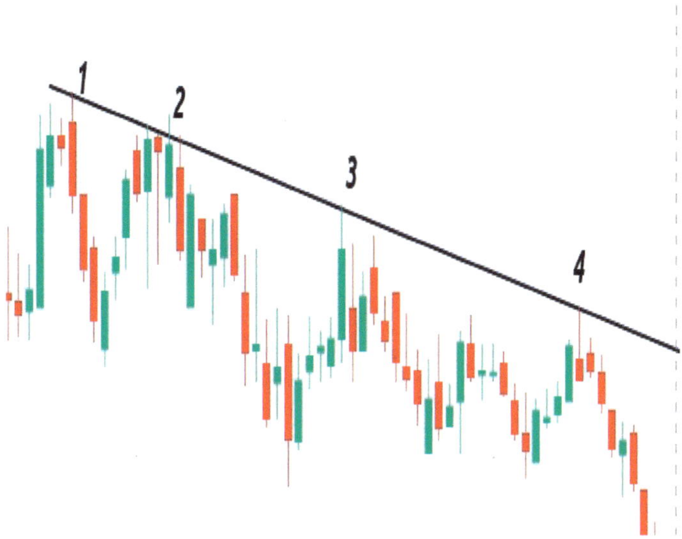

Above is an example of a trendline drawn with 4 peaks. It is called Resistance Trendline

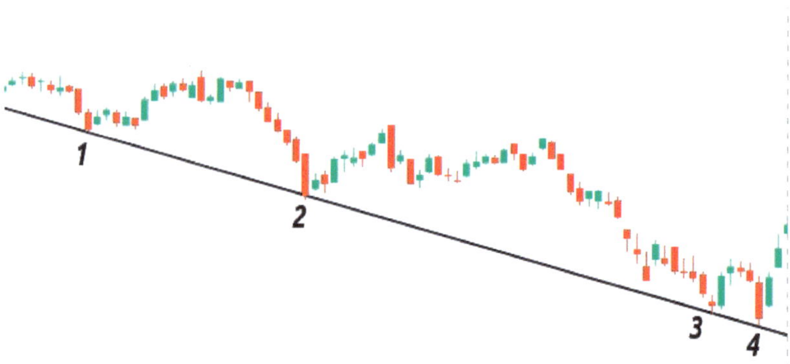

Above is an example of a trendline drawn with 4 troughs/bottom points . It is called Support Trendline

A Trendline will be more powerful when it is connected with more peaks/troughs.

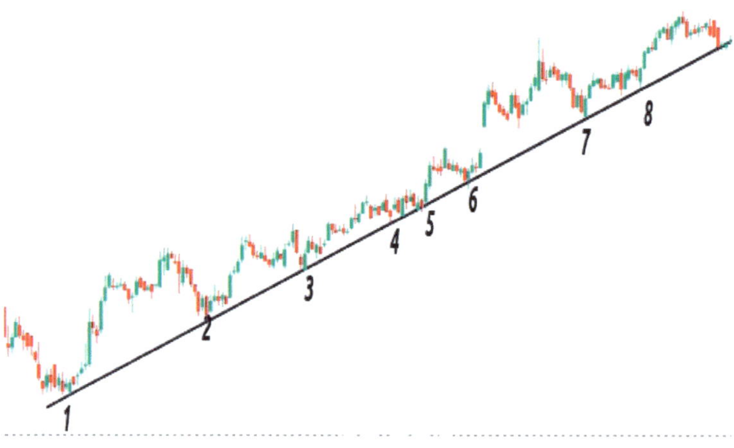

Above is an example of a trendline drawn with 8 peaks. It is a Powerful Trendline because it is respected by all the peaks. When a trendline breaks it may be the start of a strong move.

CHAPTER 3

UNLEASHING THE 200SMA MAGIC

The 200-day Simple Moving Average (SMA) is like the wise old sage of trading tools. It takes all the ups and downs of a stock's price over 200 days and smooths them out into one neat line. Think of it as a roadmap that shows you the long-term direction a stock is headed in. Whether you're a seasoned trader or just starting out, this magical line helps you see through the noise of the market and make smarter decisions. It's like having a trusted guide by your side, pointing you in the right direction as you navigate the twists and turns of investing/trading.

IMPORTANCE OF 200SMA

- **Spotting Trends**: The 200SMA helps you see the big picture. When prices are above it, it's like looking at blue skies—indicating an uptrend. When prices dip below, it's like storm clouds gathering—suggesting a downtrend.

- **Support and Resistance**: When prices get close to it, they often bounce back, giving traders a heads-up on potential reversals or continuations.

- **Reading Sentiments:** Crossovers above or below the 200SMA are like mood swings in the market.

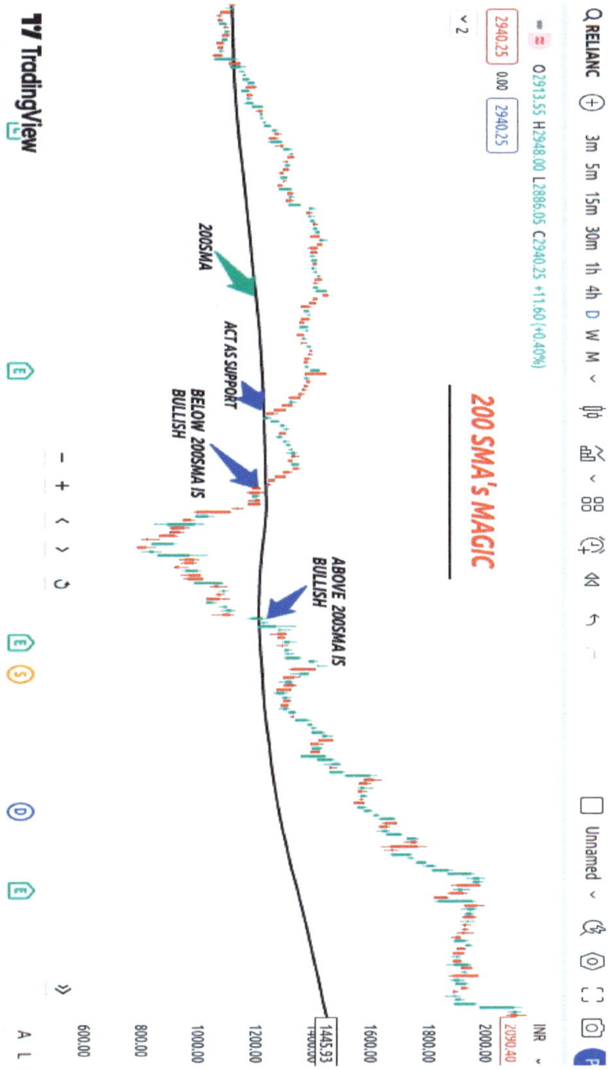
RELIANC
3m 5m 15m 30m 1h 4h D W M
O2913.55 H2948.00 L2886.05 C2940.25 +11.60 (+0.40%)
2940.25 0.00 2940.25
200 SMA's MAGIC
200SMA
ACT AS SUPPORT
BELOW 200SMA IS BULLISH
ABOVE 200SMA IS BULLISH
Unnamed
INR
2000.00
1800.00
1600.00
1445.93
1200.00
1000.00
800.00
600.00
TradingView

CHAPTER 4

MONTHLY PIVOTS - THE POWERFUL LEADING INDICATOR

WHAT ARE MONTHLY PIVOTS?

Monthly pivot points are a type of technical analysis tool used by traders to identify potential support and resistance levels for a particular asset over the course of a month. These levels are calculated based on the high, low, and close prices of the previous month.

Importance of Monthly pivots

The importance of monthly pivot points lies in their ability to provide traders with key reference points for potential price reversals, breakout levels, and areas of interest for buying or selling. They can help traders identify potential entry and exit points, set profit targets, and manage risk. Moreover they are a leading indicator that leads you to the way of consistent profit.

The calculation of monthly pivot points involves the following steps:

Pivot Point (PP): The pivot point is calculated as the average of the high, low, and close prices from the previous month.

$$PP = (\text{High}+\text{Low}+\text{Close})/3$$

Central Pivot Range (CPR): The central pivot range is a range around the pivot point that provides additional support and resistance levels. It consists of PP, Upper CPR, Lower CPR. It is calculated as follows:

- **Upper CPR**: This is calculated by adding the pivot point to the difference between the high and low of the previous month.

$$\text{Upper CPR} = PP+(\text{High}-\text{Low})$$

Lower CPR: This is calculated by subtracting the pivot point from the difference between the high and low of the previous month.

$$\text{Lower CPR} = PP-(\text{High}-\text{Low})$$

Monthly Support and Resistance Levels:

Support 1 (S1): This level is calculated as twice the pivot point minus the high of the previous month.

$$S1 = (2\times PP)-\text{High}$$

Resistance 1 (R1): This level is calculated as twice the pivot point minus the low of the previous month.

$$R1=(2\times PP)-Low$$

By using monthly pivot points, traders can gain insights into potential price movements and make more informed trading decisions. However, it's important to remember that pivot points are just one tool among many used in technical analysis, and they should be used in conjunction with other indicators and analysis techniques for comprehensive market analysis.

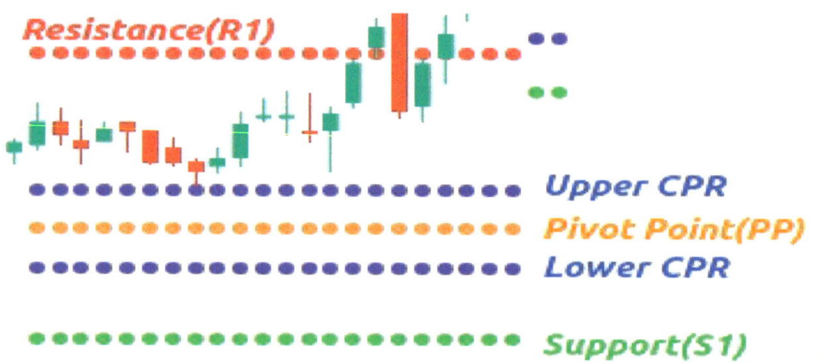

Ascending Monthly CPR

Ascending Monthly CPR happens when the latest Monthly CPR is higher than the one before it. This usually means the market is on the rise, signaling a bullish trend where prices are expected to keep going up. In this situation, it's best to take long positions, meaning you're betting on prices going higher.

Ascending Monthly CPR (Bullish Outlook)

Descending Monthly CPR

Descending Monthly CPR occurs when the latest Monthly CPR is lower than the previous one. This points to a downward trend in the market, indicating a bearish outlook where prices are likely to fall further. In such cases, it's advisable to take short positions, meaning you're betting on prices going lower.

Descending Monthly CPR(Bearish Outlook)

Inside Monthly CPR

The "inside monthly CPR" occurs when the monthly central pivot range (CPR) of a stock is entirely contained within the boundaries of the previous month's CPR. This situation arises when the share price exhibits a narrow trading range.

Decoding the Mystery of Narrow Monthly CPR in Swing Trading

The difference between the highest and lowest prices of the previous month is pretty small. That's what we call a Narrow Monthly Central Pivot Range (CPR). It tells us that the market's trading range is tighter compared to other months when the price gap is bigger.

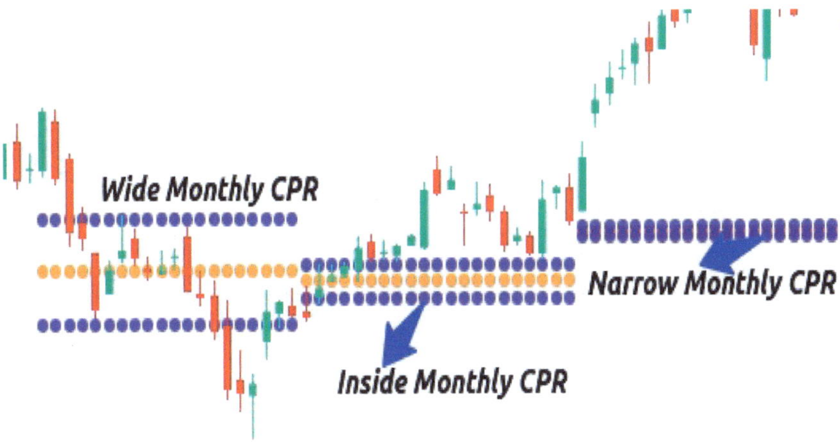

When we see a narrow monthly CPR, it could mean a few things. It might suggest that the market is less bumpy, maybe unsure about which way to go. This could lead traders to tweak their strategies, keeping an eye out for potential breakthroughs or changes in direction at specific CPR levels.

But remember, while a narrow monthly CPR gives us useful clues about the market, it's not the only thing to consider. Savvy traders take into account other factors too, like a detective piecing together clues to solve a mystery. So let's dive in and explore how we can use narrow monthly CPR to make smarter trading decisions !

Unlocking High Probability Setups:

Chart patterns, whether it's an accumulation phase or a distribution phase, provide valuable insights into market sentiment. However, the key to success lies in identifying breakout phases within these patterns. This is where the monthly CPR comes into play. By incorporating the monthly CPR into our analysis, we increase our probability of identifying high-quality setups while minimizing false signals.

PART-2

FOUR SWING TRADING STRATEGIES

STRATEGY 1

PATTERN BREAKOUT WITH NARROW & INSIDE MONTHLY CPR

To implement this strategy, we start by screening for stocks with narrow or Inside Monthly CPR using tools like Chartink. These stocks represent a potential breakout opportunity. Once we have a list of candidate stocks, we then look for additional confirmation through chart patterns such as triangle patterns or channel patterns. **When a stock meets both criteria – narrow/Inside Monthly CPR and a chart pattern – we have a high probability setup on our hands.**

One of the key advantages of this strategy is the ability to manage risk effectively. With minimal stop-loss levels, either at the boundaries of the chart pattern or the monthly CPR, we can limit potential losses while maximizing upside potential. This ensures that even if the trade doesn't go as planned, the impact on our overall portfolio is controlled.

With this strategy, we position ourselves to capitalize on sharp moves in either direction. Whether it's an upside breakout or a downside breakdown, the combination of monthly CPR and chart patterns helps us identify and capitalize on these opportunities.

By combining the power of Monthly CPR with chart patterns, we unlock a high probability strategy for swing trading. This approach not only helps us navigate through market uncertainties but also positions us to capitalize on sharp moves with minimal risk. Whether you're a seasoned trader or just starting out, mastering this strategy can significantly enhance your trading performance.

In the following pages, we'll explore real-world examples that demonstrate the effectiveness of this strategy. Through these case studies, you'll gain a deeper understanding of how to apply this approach in your own trading endeavors.

STRATEGY1 - CASE STUDY 1

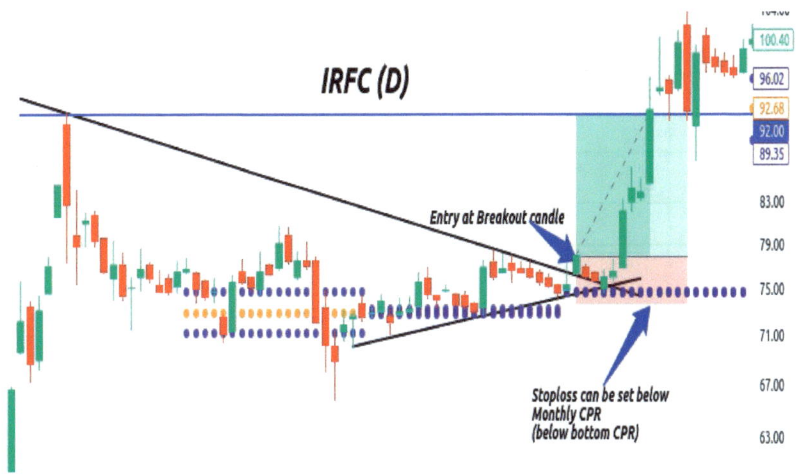

IRFC

- The stock has a symmetrical triangle formation with a narrow and inside monthly CPR (It is a high probable setup)
- Entry at 77
- Stop loss at 74.25 (bottom monthly CPR at 74.65 ,add a little bit buffer to it and placed the SL)
- Risk is 2.75 points hence the reward must be at least two times of the risk taken.
- In this case we can set the reward at 92 which is the existing all time high at that time. Risk reward ratio here is 1 : 3.5

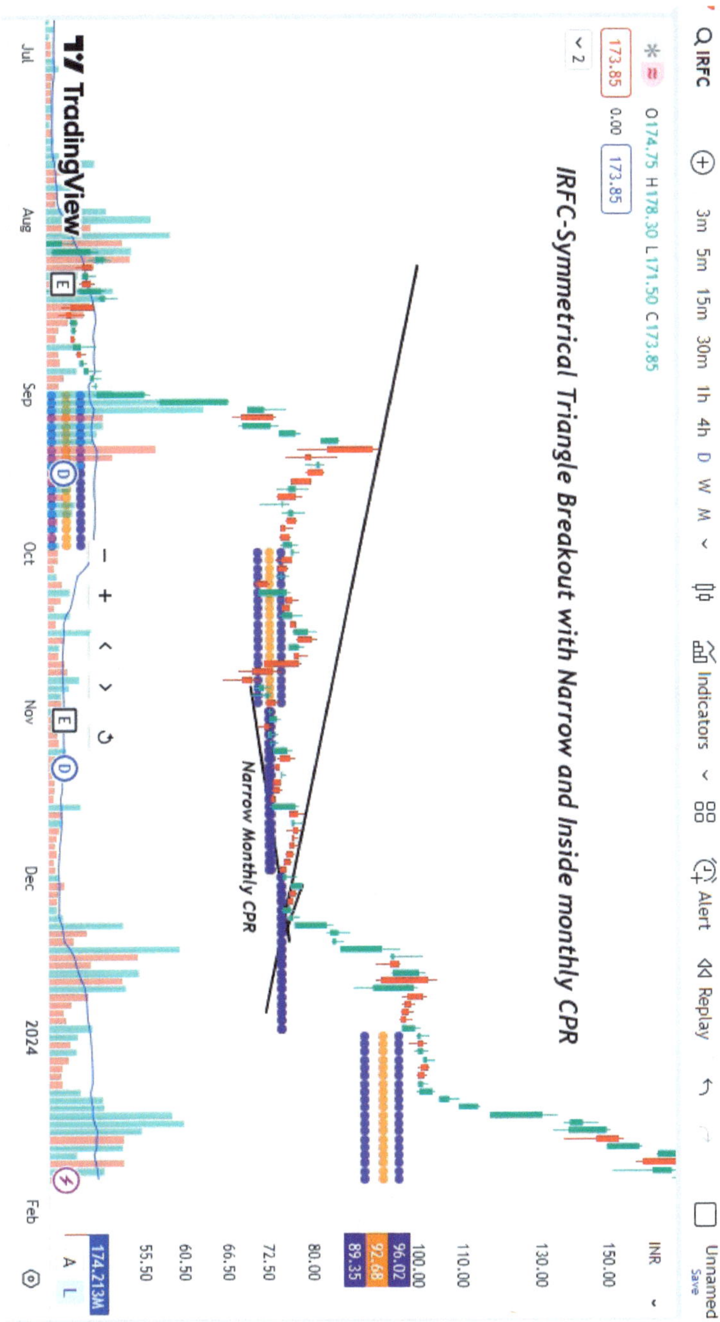
IRFC
O174.75 H178.30 L171.50 C173.85
173.85
0.00
173.85
IRFC-Symmetrical Triangle Breakout with Narrow and Inside monthly CPR
Narrow Monthly CPR
Indicators
Alert
Replay
Unnamed
TradingView
INR
150.00
130.00
110.00
100.00
96.02
92.68
89.35
80.00
72.50
66.50
60.50
55.50
174.213M
Jul
Aug
Sep
Oct
Nov
Dec
2024
Feb

CASE STUDY 2

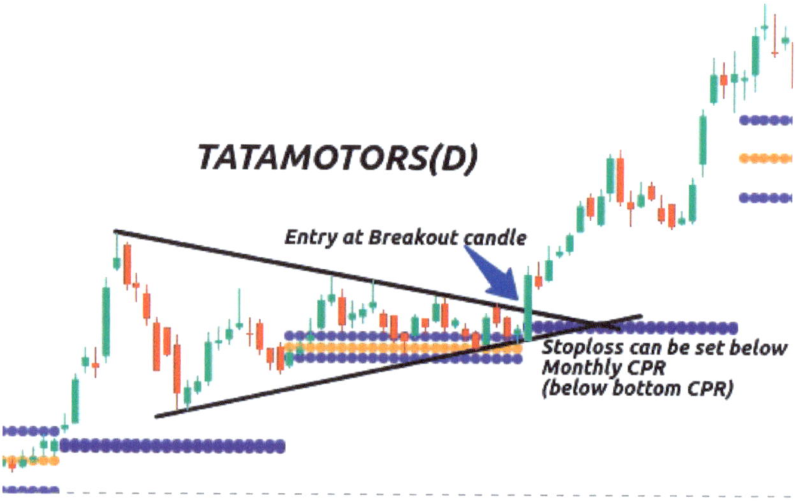

TATAMOTORS

- The stock has a symmetrical triangle formation with a narrow and inside monthly CPR (It is a high probable setup)
- Entry at 108.75
- Stop loss at 104.75 (bottom monthly CPR at 104.85 ,add a little bit buffer to it and placed the SL)
- Risk is 4 points hence the reward must be at least two times of the risk taken. You can ride the rally until the momentum losses. When we achieve a reward of 2 times of the risk taken, and momentum is still there, then you can book partial profit or place a trailing Stop Loss.

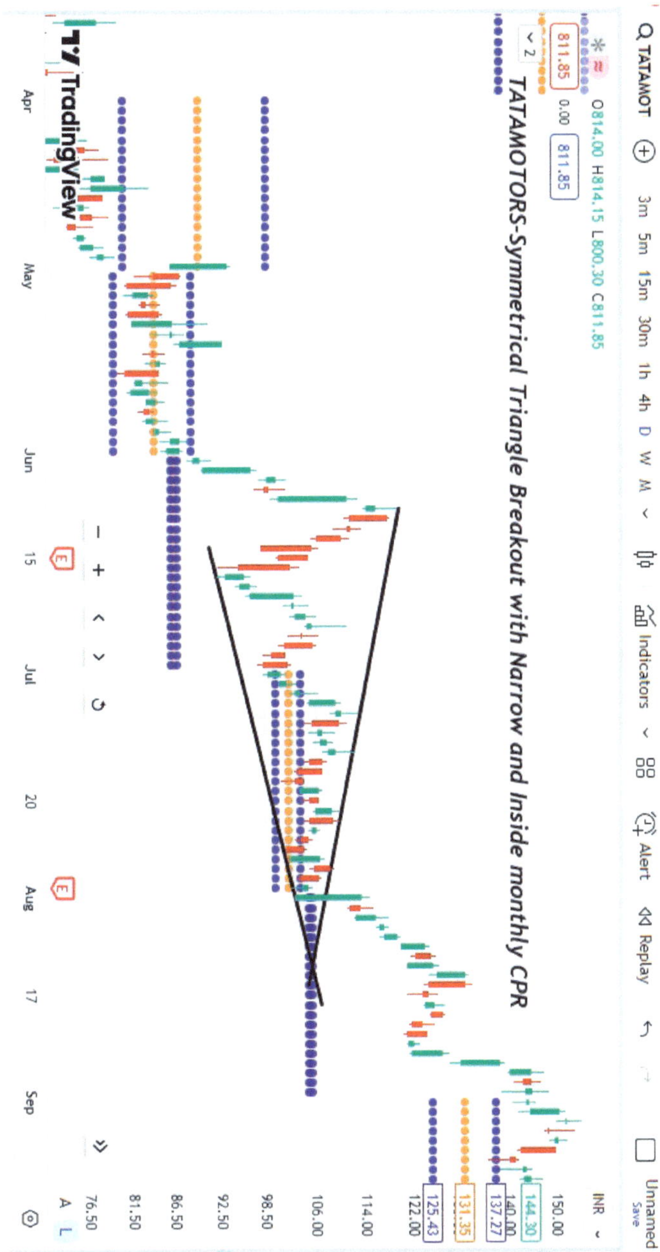
TATAMOT
O814.00 H814.15 L800.30 C811.85
811.85 0.00 811.85
3m 5m 15m 30m 1h 4h D W M
Indicators
Alert
Replay
Unnamed
Save
TATAMOTORS-Symmetrical Triangle Breakout with Narrow and Inside monthly CPR
INR
150.00
144.30
140.00
137.27
131.35
125.43
122.00
114.00
106.00
98.50
92.50
86.50
81.50
76.50
Apr
May
Jun
15
Jul
20
Aug
17
Sep
TradingView

CASE STUDY 3

APOLLO

- The stock has a channel pattern formation with a narrow and inside monthly CPR (It is a high probable setup)
- Entry at 60
- Stop loss at 56.5 (bottom monthly CPR at 56.65 ,add a little bit buffer to it and placed the SL)
- Risk is 3.5 points hence the reward must be at least two times of the risk taken. You can ride the rally until the momentum losses. When we achieve a reward of 2 times of the risk taken, and momentum is still there, then you can book partial profit or place a trailing Stop Loss.

APOLLO
3m 5m 15m 30m 1h 4h D W M
Indicators
Alert
Replay
O118.90 H119.95 L118.00 C118.90
118.90 0.00 118.90
Channel pattern breakout with Narrow and Inside monthly CPR
INR
131.75
118.90
110.00
95.00
85.85
80.30
74.75
71.00
63.50
56.00
50.00
44.00
39.00
Mar Apr May Jun Jul Aug Sep Oct Nov
TradingView

CASE STUDY 4

IRCON

- The stock has a Ascending Triangle formation with a narrow monthly CPR
- Here there is two entries
- Breakout entry at 187
- If you miss the breakout entry there is a retest entry opportunity at 180
- Stop loss at 169

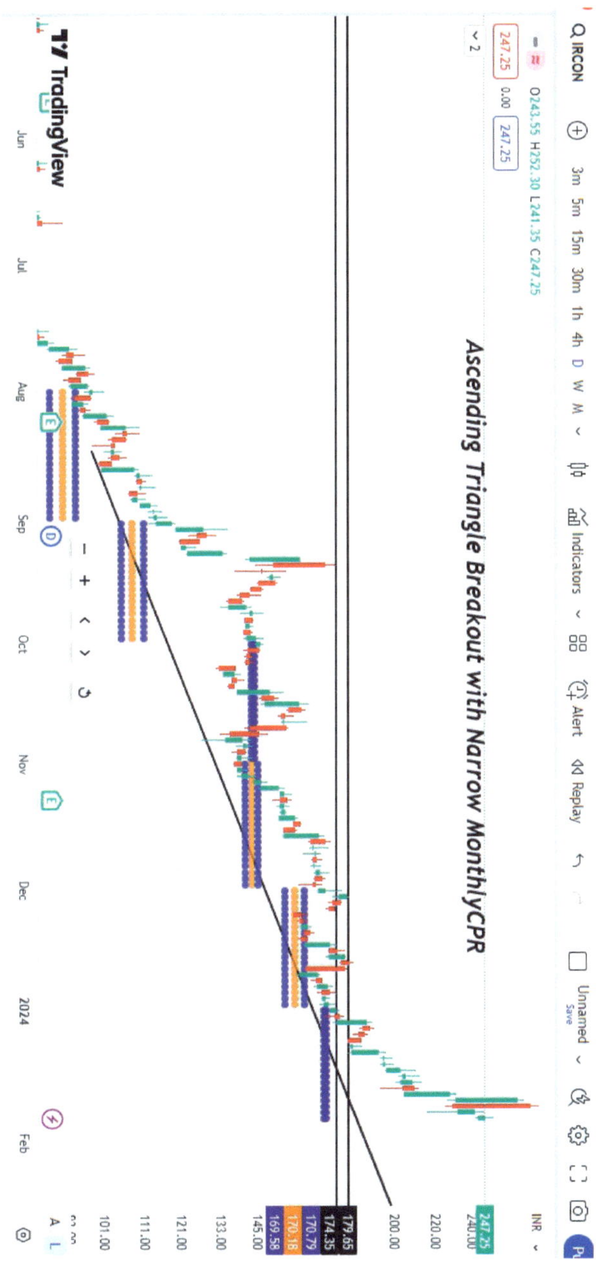
IRCON
O243.55 H252.30 L241.35 C247.25
Indicators
Alert
Replay
Unnamed
Ascending Triangle Breakout with Narrow MonthlyCPR
INR
247.25
240.00
220.00
200.00
179.65
174.35
170.79
170.18
169.58
145.00
133.00
121.00
111.00
101.00
Jun
Jul
Aug
Sep
Oct
Nov
Dec
2024
Feb
TradingView

CASE STUDY 5

BSE

- The stock has a Symmetrical Triangle pattern formation with a narrow monthly CPR
- Entry at 412
- Stop loss at 402 (place SL below bottom monthly CPR)
- Risk is 10 points hence the reward must be at least two times of the risk taken.In this case we can set reward at the nearest resistance i.e., 470
- Risk reward ratio here is 1 : 5.8

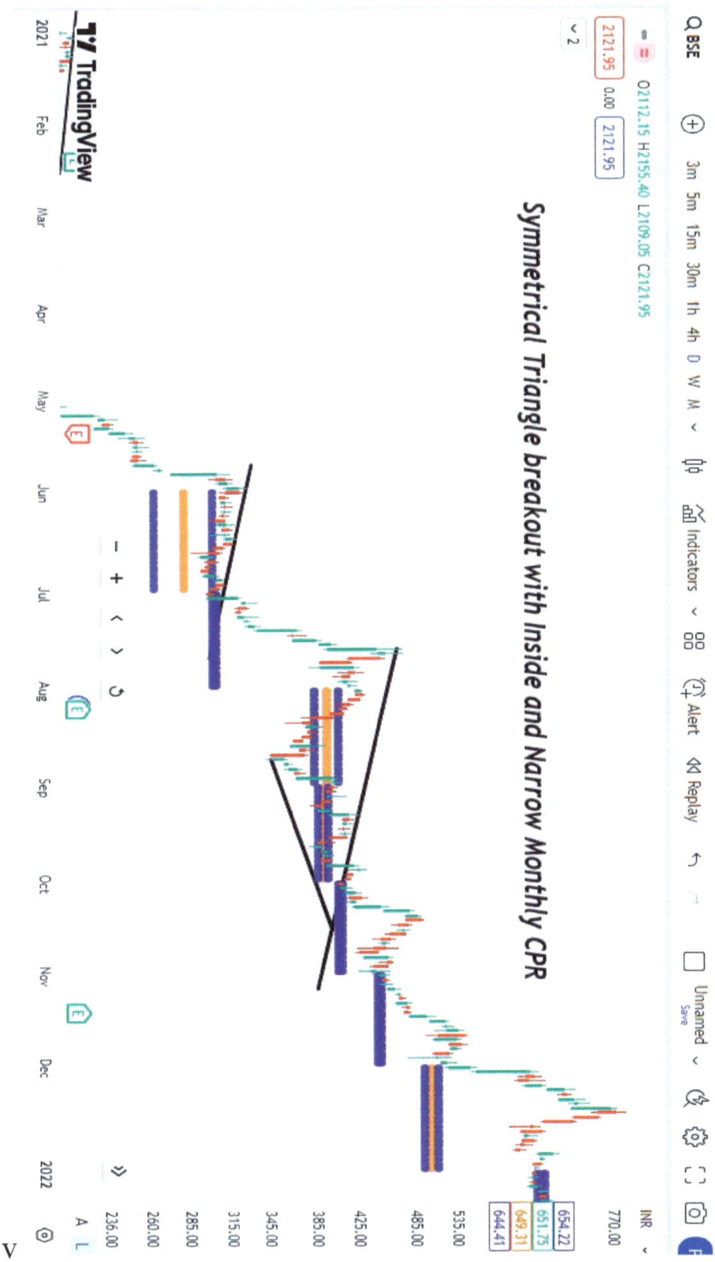
Symmetrical Triangle breakout with Inside and Narrow Monthly CPR
BSE
O2112.15 H2155.40 L2109.05 C2121.95
2121.95 0.00 2121.95
TradingView
2021 Feb Mar Apr May Jun Jul Aug Sep Oct Nov Dec 2022
770.00 654.22 651.75 649.31 644.41 535.00 485.00 425.00 385.00 345.00 315.00 285.00 260.00 236.00
INR

CASE STUDY 6

SOLARINDS

- The stock has a symmetrical triangle formation with a narrow and inside monthly CPR (It is a high probable setup)
- But in this case during the narrow CPR month,breakout doesn't happen. If breakout does not happen during the narrow CPR month,we can expect a high probable breakout in the next month.
- Entry at 2860
- Stop loss at 2745 (place SL below bottom Monthly CPR)

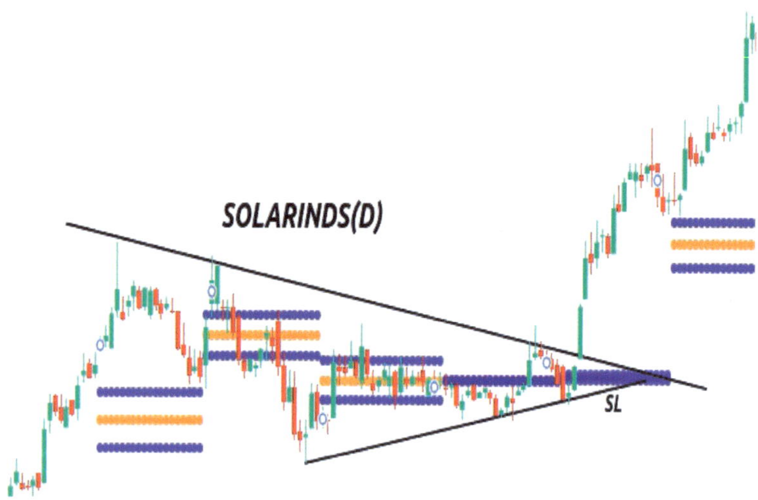

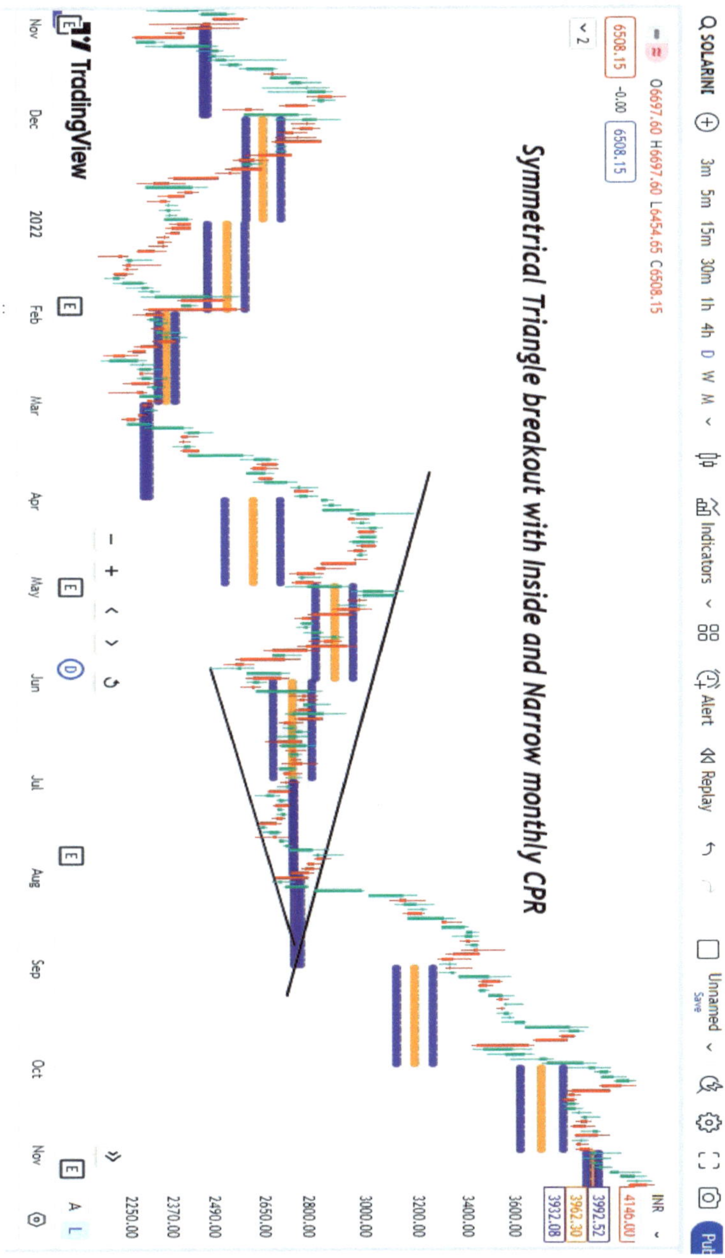
Q SOLARINI
O6697.60 H6697.60 L6454.65 C6508.15
6508.15 -0.00 6508.15
3m 5m 15m 30m 1h 4h D W M
Indicators
Alert
Replay
Unnamed
Save
Symmetrical Triangle breakout with Inside and Narrow monthly CPR
INR
4146.00
3992.52
3962.30
3932.08
3600.00
3400.00
3200.00
3000.00
2800.00
2650.00
2490.00
2370.00
2250.00
Nov
Dec
2022
Feb
Mar
Apr
May
Jun
Jul
Aug
Sep
Oct
Nov
TradingView

CASE STUDY 7

BLS

- The stock has a symmetrical triangle formation with a narrow and inside monthly CPR (It is a high probable setup)
- Entry at 62.5
- Stop loss at 57.5 (place SL below bottom monthly CPR)
- Risk is 5 points hence the reward must be at least two times of the risk taken. You can ride the rally until the momentum losses. When we achieve a reward of 2 times of the risk taken, and momentum is still there, then you can book partial profit or place a trailing Stop Loss.

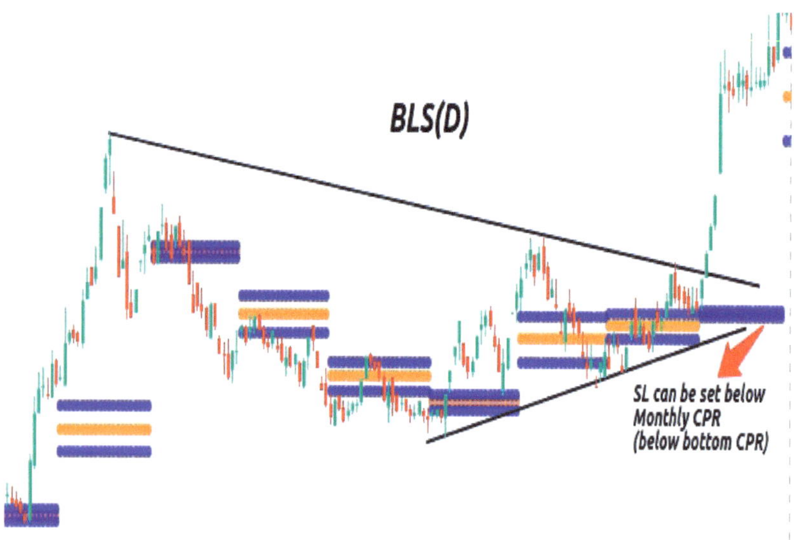

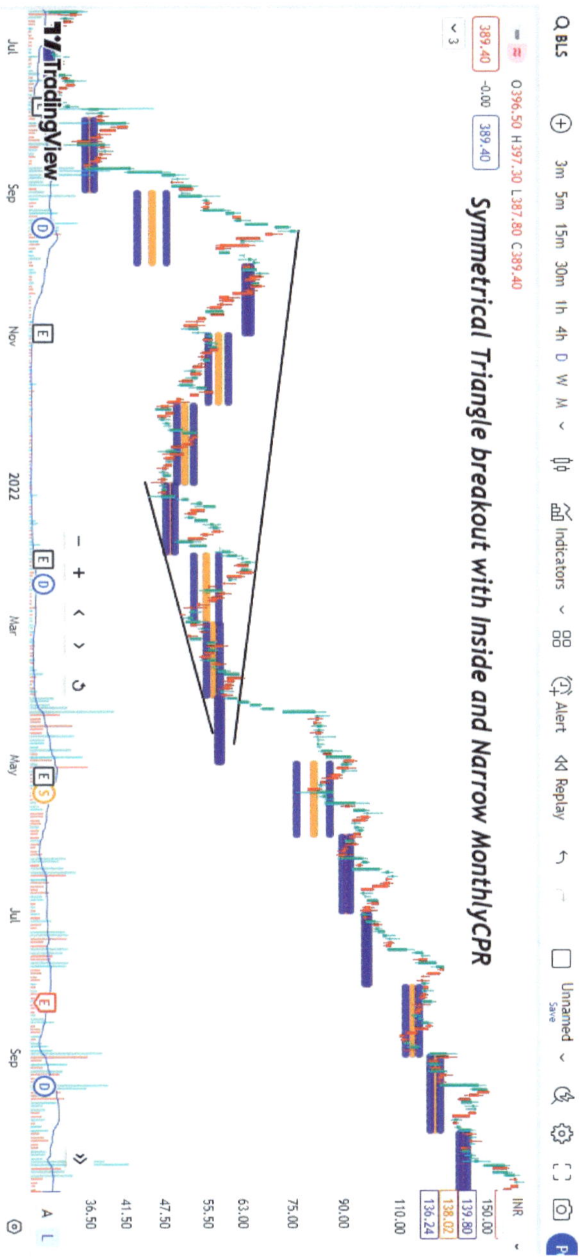
Symmetrical Triangle breakout with Inside and Narrow MonthlyCPR
BLS
O396.50 H397.30 L387.80 C389.40
389.40 -0.00 389.40
TradingView
Jul
Sep
Nov
2022
Mar
May
Jul
Sep
INR
150.00
139.80
138.02
136.24
110.00
90.00
75.00
63.00
55.50
47.50
41.50
36.50

CASE STUDY 8

ADANIENT

In this case, there are two entries. One is a long entry and the other is a short entry.

Long Entry

- The stock has a symmetrical triangle formation with a narrow and inside monthly CPR (It is a high probable setup)

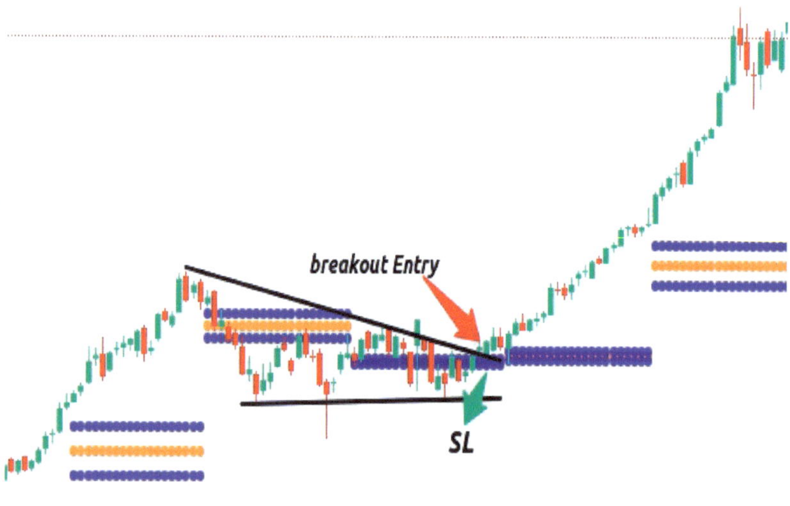

- Entry at 2200
- Stop loss at 2125 (place SL below bottom monthly CPR)
- Risk is 75 points hence the reward must be at least two times of the risk taken. In this case we can

achieve more than 1000 points in a short span by just riding the rally.

SHORT ENTRY

- In this case we have channel pattern breakdown

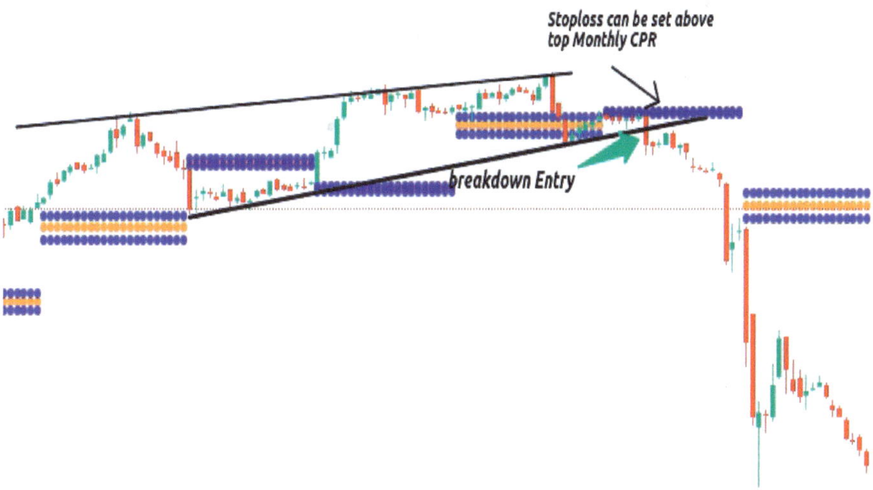

- Entry at 3630
- Stop loss at 3930 (place SL below bottom monthly CPR)
- Risk is 75 points hence the reward must be at least two times of the risk taken. In this case we can achieve more than 2500 points in a short span by just riding the rally.

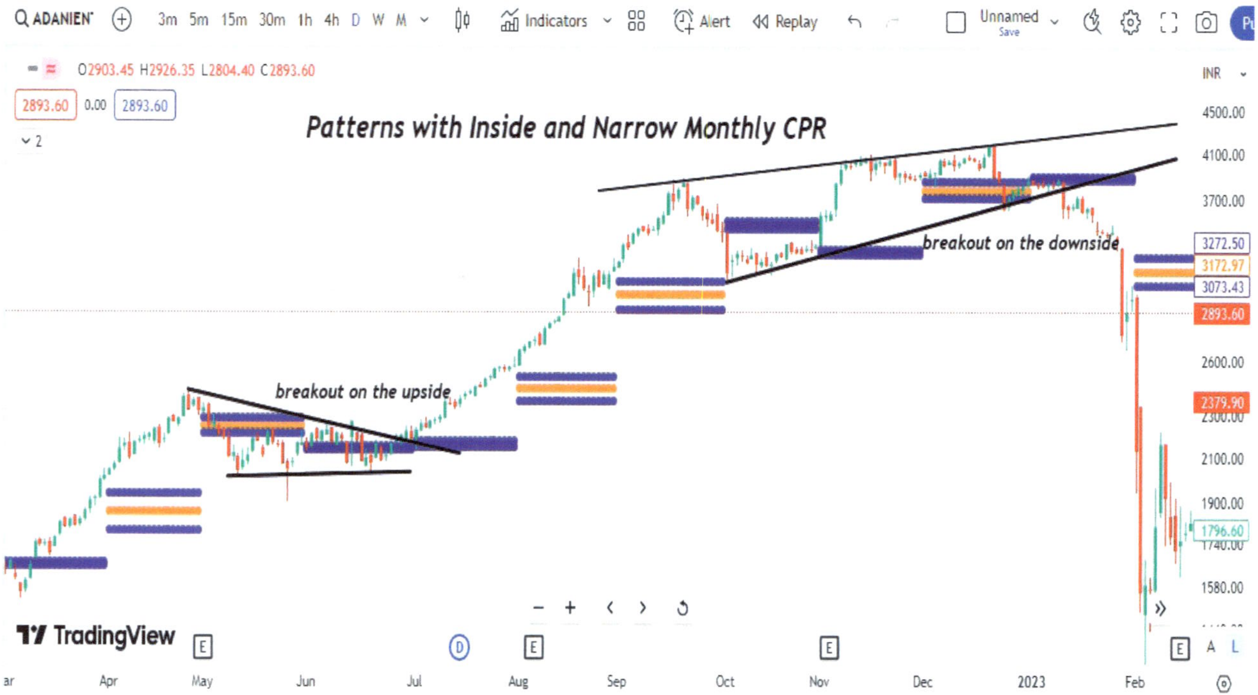

ADANIENT
3m 5m 15m 30m 1h 4h D W M
Indicators
Alert
Replay
Unnamed
Save
O2903.45 H2926.35 L2804.40 C2893.60
2893.60 0.00 2893.60
INR
Patterns with Inside and Narrow Monthly CPR
breakout on the upside
breakout on the downside
4500.00
4100.00
3700.00
3272.50
3172.97
3073.43
2893.60
2600.00
2379.90
2100.00
1900.00
1796.60
1580.00
TradingView
Apr
May
Jun
Jul
Aug
Sep
Oct
Nov
Dec
2023
Feb

STRATEGY 2

TRENDLINE BREAKOUT + 200SMA BREAKOUT

Imagine combining the power of trendline breakouts with the magic of the 200SMA. It's like mixing your favorite superhero powers to create an unstoppable force in the trading universe.

Here's how it works:

- **Spotting Breakouts**: Keep an eye on stocks that break key trendlines. If a stock breaks above, it's like a rocket ready to launch. If it breaks below, it's like a submarine diving deep.
- **Checking 200SMA**: Once you spot a trendline breakout, see where the stock's price stands relative to the 200SMA. If it's below, it's like waiting for the perfect moment to strike.
- **Confirmation is Key**: Sometimes, the trendline and 200SMA align perfectly, giving you a double confirmation signal—like two thumbs up for a trade. But trendline breakout subsequent to 200SMA breakout is not that much preferable. Of course it works, but not a high probable setup.

- **Executing the Trade**: Wait for the price to break above the 200SMA after confirming the trendline breakout. It's like waiting for the right moment to unleash your trading powers.
- **Managing Risks**: Always play it safe by setting stop-loss orders to protect your gains and minimize losses. It's like wearing a seatbelt while driving—you never know when you might hit a bump in the road.

The Trendline + 200SMA Breakout strategy isn't just another trading tactic; it's a winning formula for swing traders and long-term investors alike. By combining the strengths of trendline breakouts with the magic of the 200SMA, you're not just riding the waves; you're mastering the art of trading in the ever-changing market seas. So, gear up, stay patient, and get ready to ride the trendline and 200SMA waves to trading success! 🚀

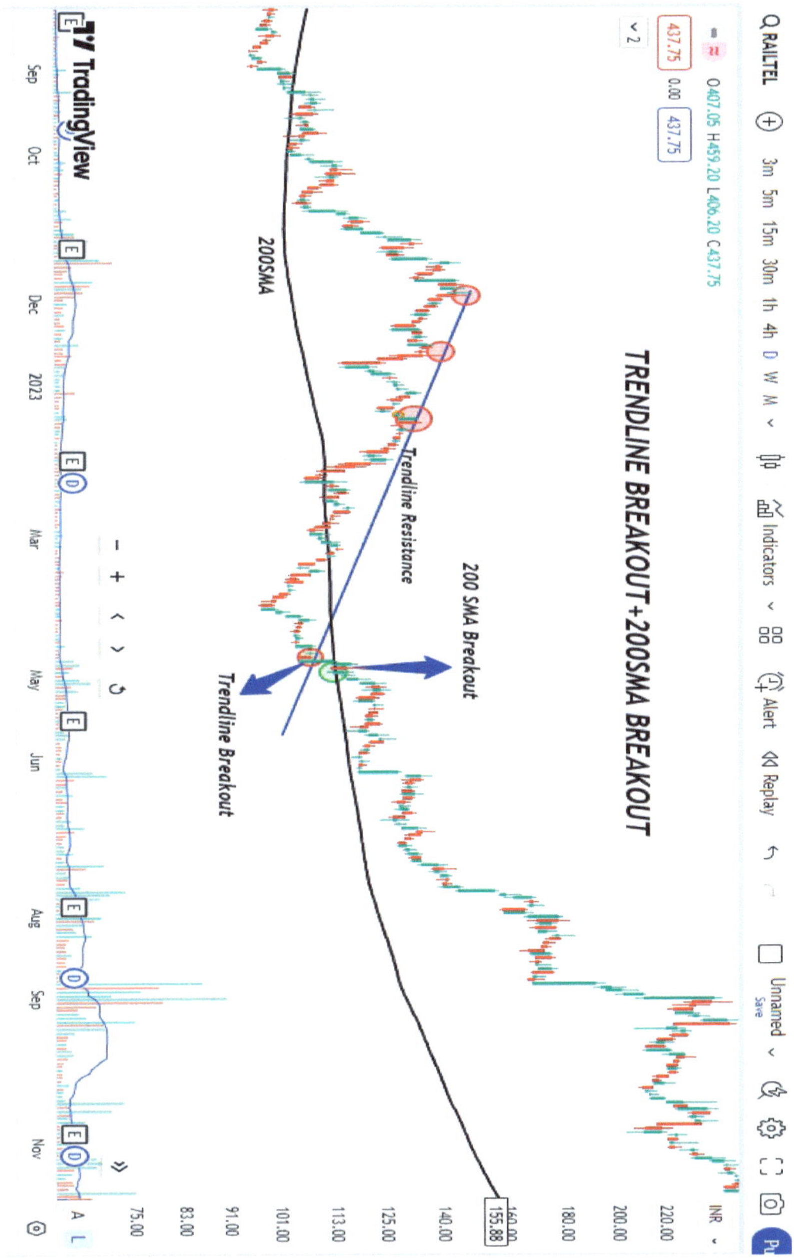
RAILTEL
O407.05 H459.20 L406.20 C437.75
TRENDLINE BREAKOUT+200SMA BREAKOUT
Trendline Resistance
200 SMA Breakout
Trendline Breakout
200SMA
TradingView

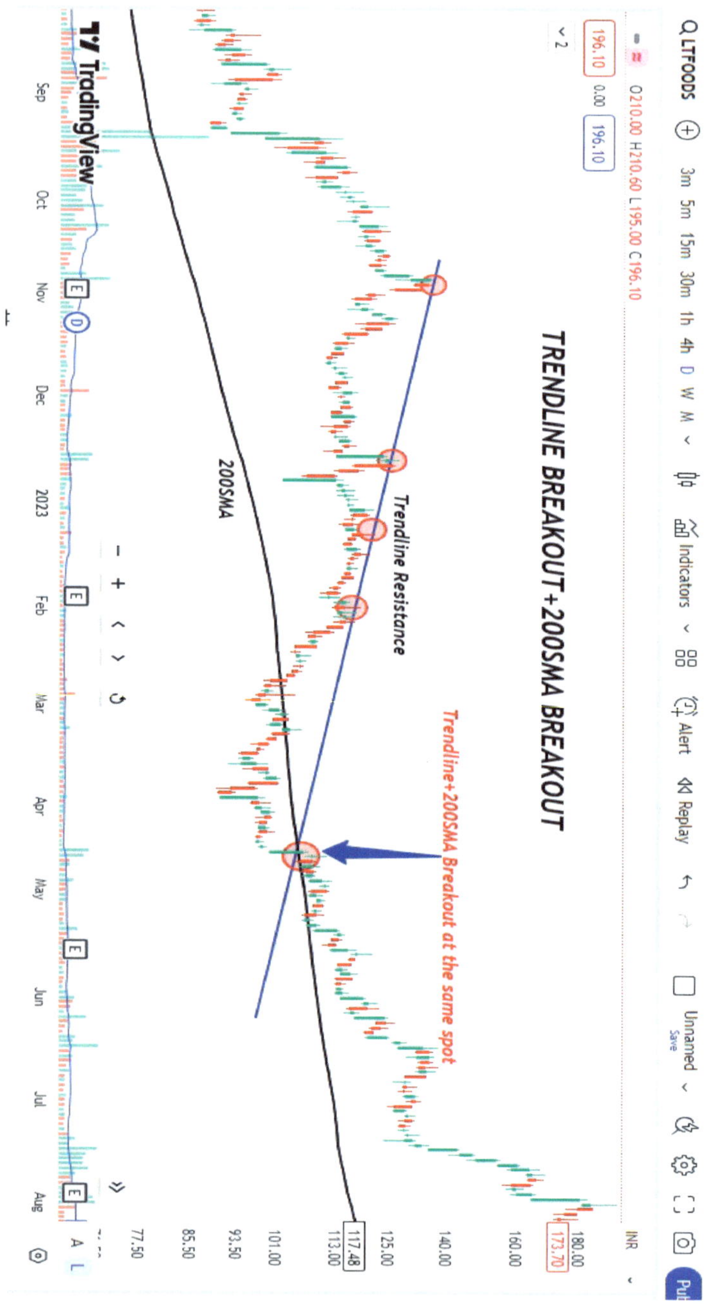
LTFOODS
TRENDLINE BREAKOUT+200SMA BREAKOUT
Trendline Resistance
200SMA
Trendline+200SMA Breakout at the same spot
TradingView

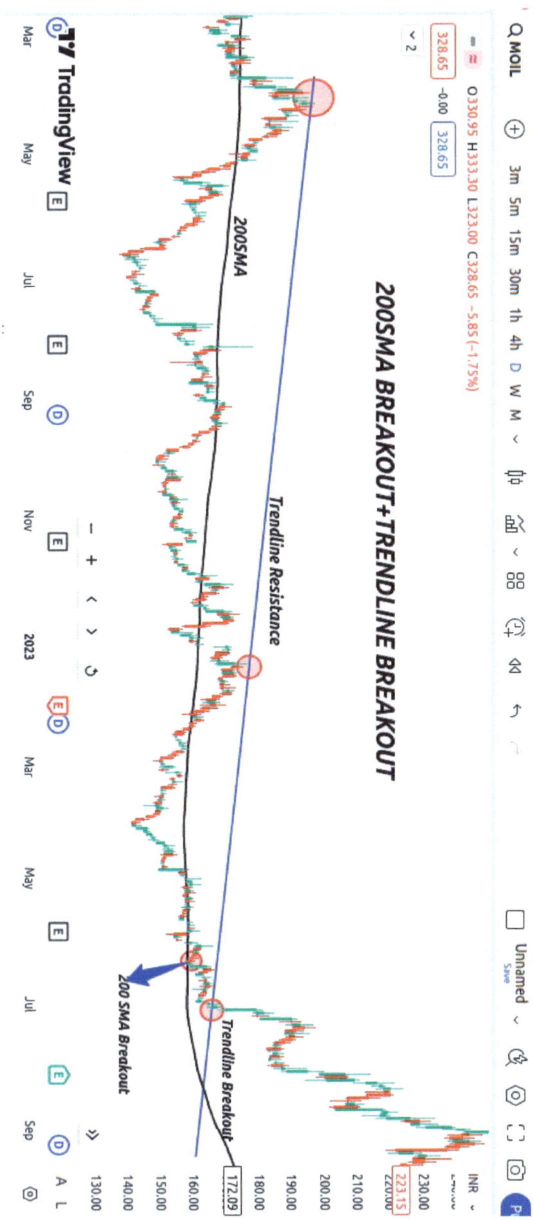
MOIL
O330.95 H333.30 L323.00 C328.65 −5.85 (−1.75%)
200SMA BREAKOUT+TRENDLINE BREAKOUT
200SMA
Trendline Resistance
Trendline Breakout
200 SMA Breakout
TradingView

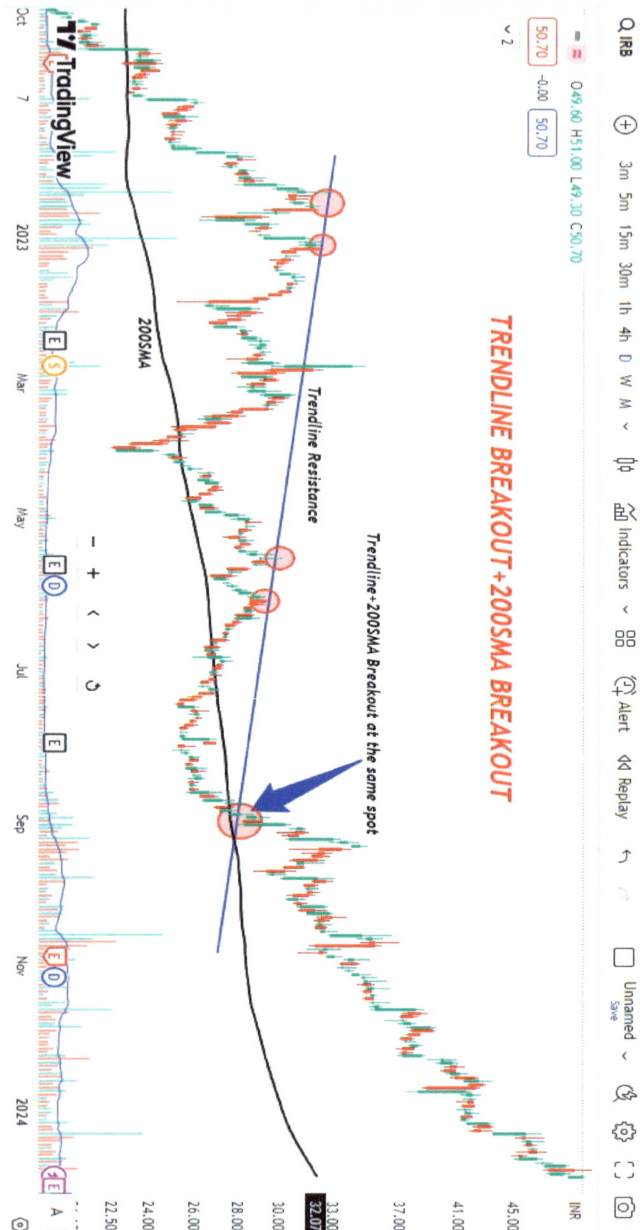
TRENDLINE BREAKOUT+200SMA BREAKOUT
Trendline+200SMA Breakout at the same spot
Trendline Resistance
200SMA
TradingView

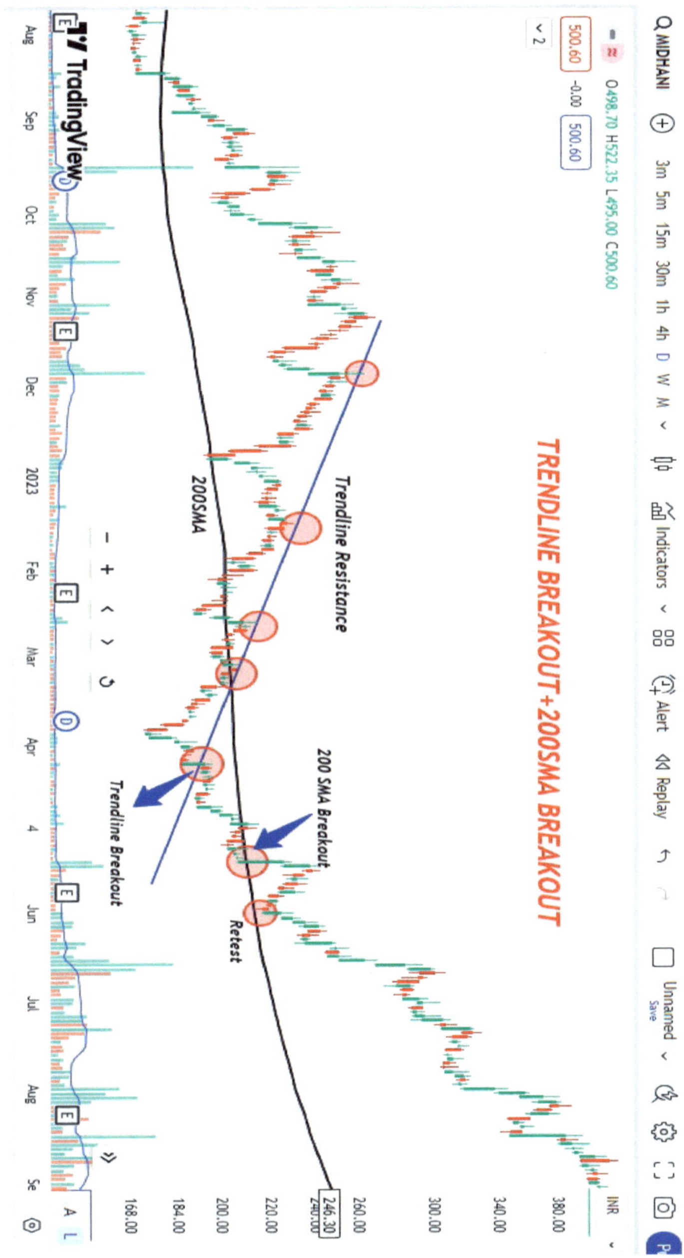
MIDHANI
O498.70 H522.35 L495.00 C500.60
TRENDLINE BREAKOUT+200SMA BREAKOUT
Trendline Resistance
200SMA
200 SMA Breakout
Trendline Breakout
Retest
TradingView

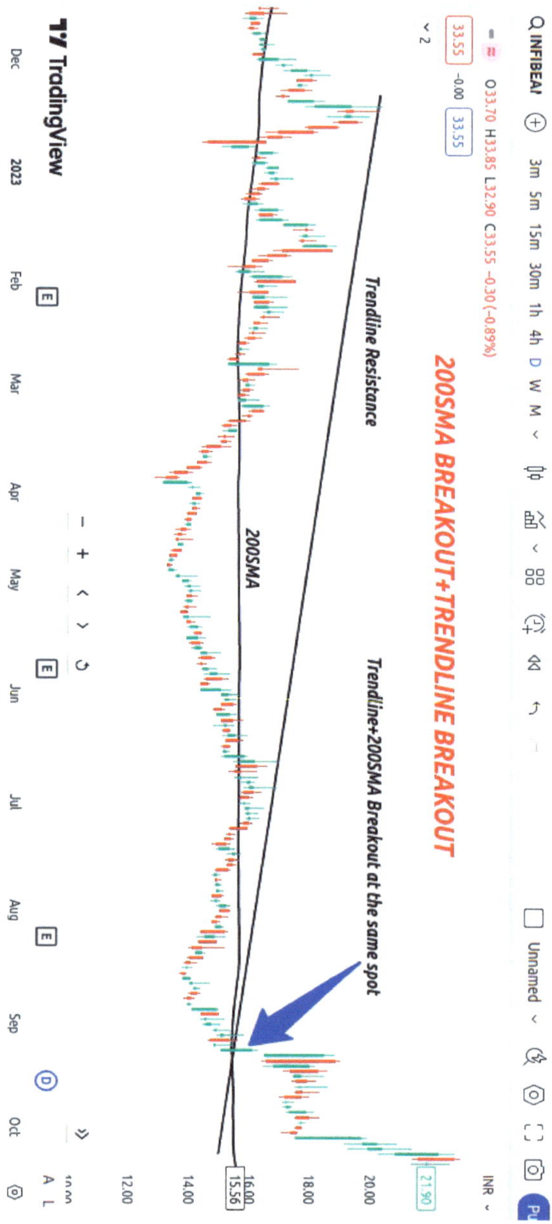

200SMA BREAKOUT+TRENDLINE BREAKOUT
Trendline Resistance
200SMA
Trendline+200SMA Breakout at the same spot

STRATEGY 3

PULLBACK TO MONTHLY CPR STRATEGY

Have you ever noticed how sometimes when we try to jump into a trade when a stock breaks out, it doesn't always go the way we expect? We might encounter fakeouts, get in too late, or feel overwhelmed by emotions. But there's a strategy that can help us navigate through all of that. It's all about managing our risks and making sure the potential rewards are worth it. And you know what? Most of the time, it works out really well! By focusing on this one strategy, you can set yourself up for success in swing trading.

Remember when we talked about those different phases the market goes through? In those earlier chapters, we covered the basics of spotting those phases on a chart. I even gave you some examples to help you out. But here's the thing: to really master this strategy, you've gotta practice identifying those phases on your own. That's where the real magic happens!

So, picture this: **a stock breaks out of an accumulation phase, and we're all set to jump in. But instead of rushing in, we wait for it to take a little breather and pull back to the Monthly CPR (Central Pivot Range). It's like lining up the perfect shot, just like a sniper would. And here's the best part: even if you miss that first opportunity,**

there are still chances to get in on the action in the following months when the stock pulls back to the next month's CPR. That's your second entry. And if you're lucky, you can even get a third entry in the third month when you're in an actual markup phase.

By using this strategy, we can grab all the profits that come with a markup phase. And guess what? You can even use this same strategy when you're shorting futures markets. It's like having a secret weapon in your trading arsenal!

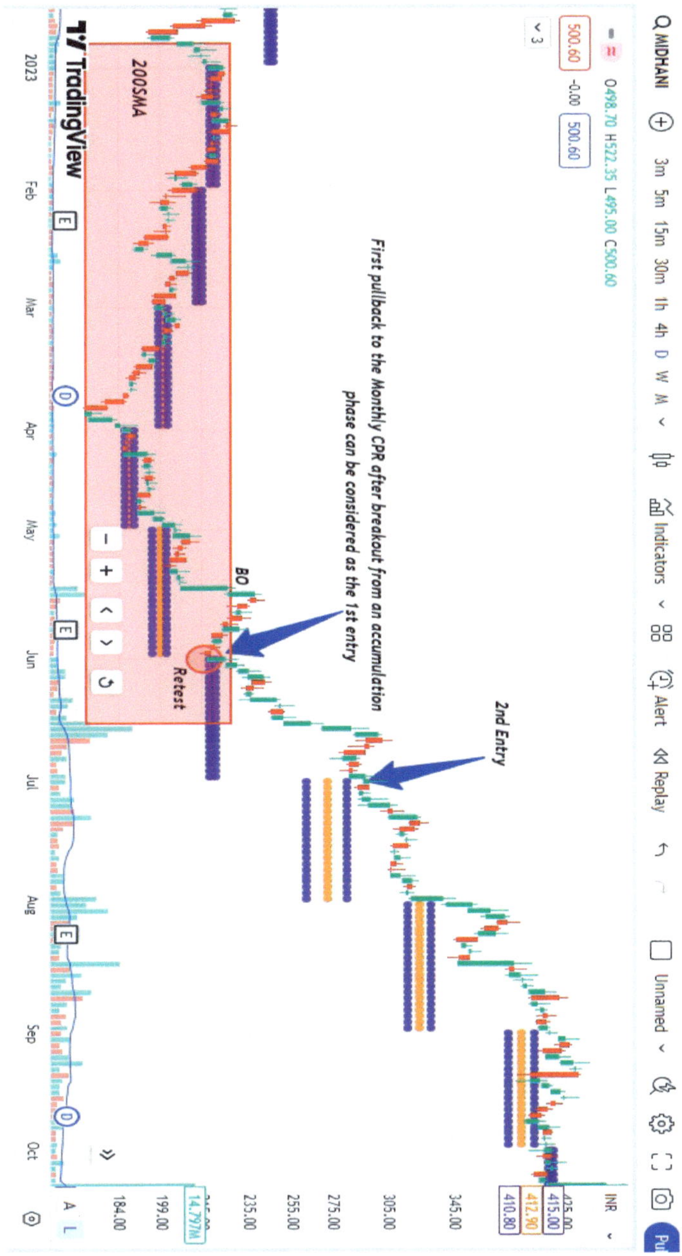
MIDHANI
First pullback to the Monthly CPR after breakout from an accumulation phase can be considered as the 1st entry
2nd Entry
BO
Retest
200SMA
TradingView

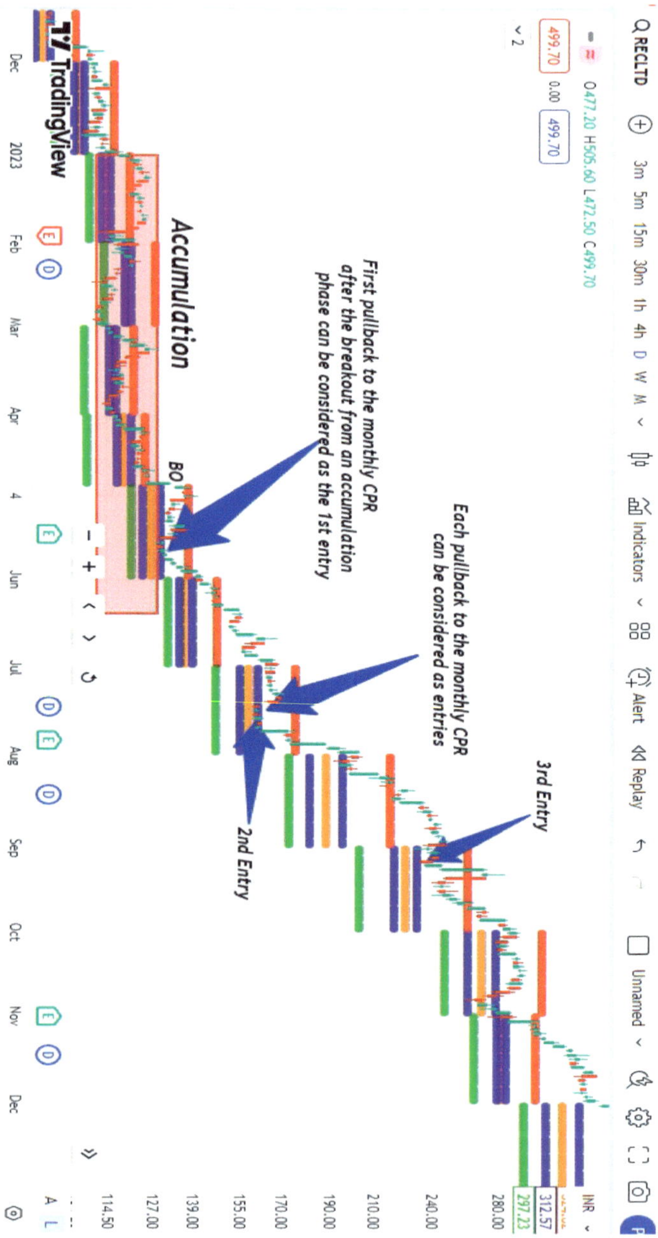
RECLTD
O477.20 H505.60 L472.50 C499.70
499.70
0.00
499.70
3m 5m 15m 30m 1h 4h D W M
Indicators
Alert
Replay
Unnamed
INR
312.57
297.23
280.00
240.00
210.00
190.00
170.00
155.00
139.00
127.00
114.50
Accumulation
BO
First pullback to the monthly CPR after the breakout from an accumulation phase can be considered as the 1st entry
Each pullback to the monthly CPR can be considered as entries
2nd Entry
3rd Entry
TradingView
Dec
2023
Feb
Mar
Apr
4
Jun
Jul
Aug
Sep
Oct
Nov
Dec

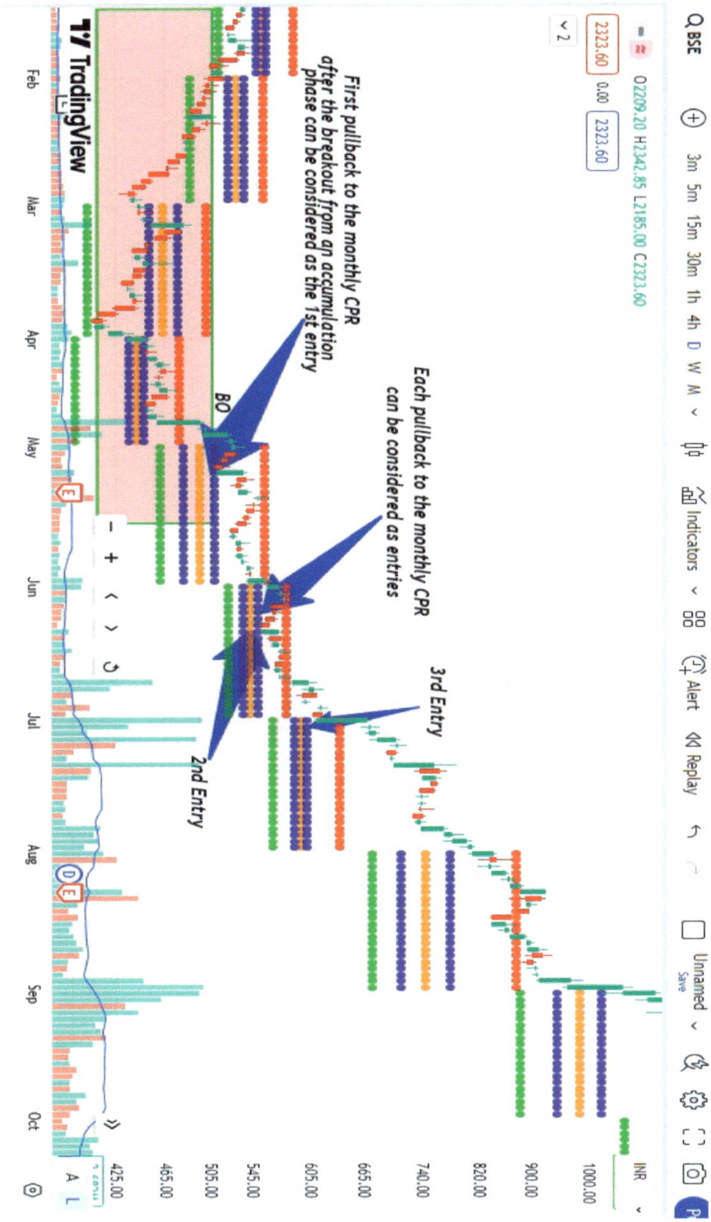
BSE
O2209.20 H2342.85 L2185.00 C2323.60
First pullback to the monthly CPR after the breakout from an accumulation phase can be considered as the 1st entry
BO
Each pullback to the monthly CPR can be considered as entries
2nd Entry
3rd Entry
TradingView

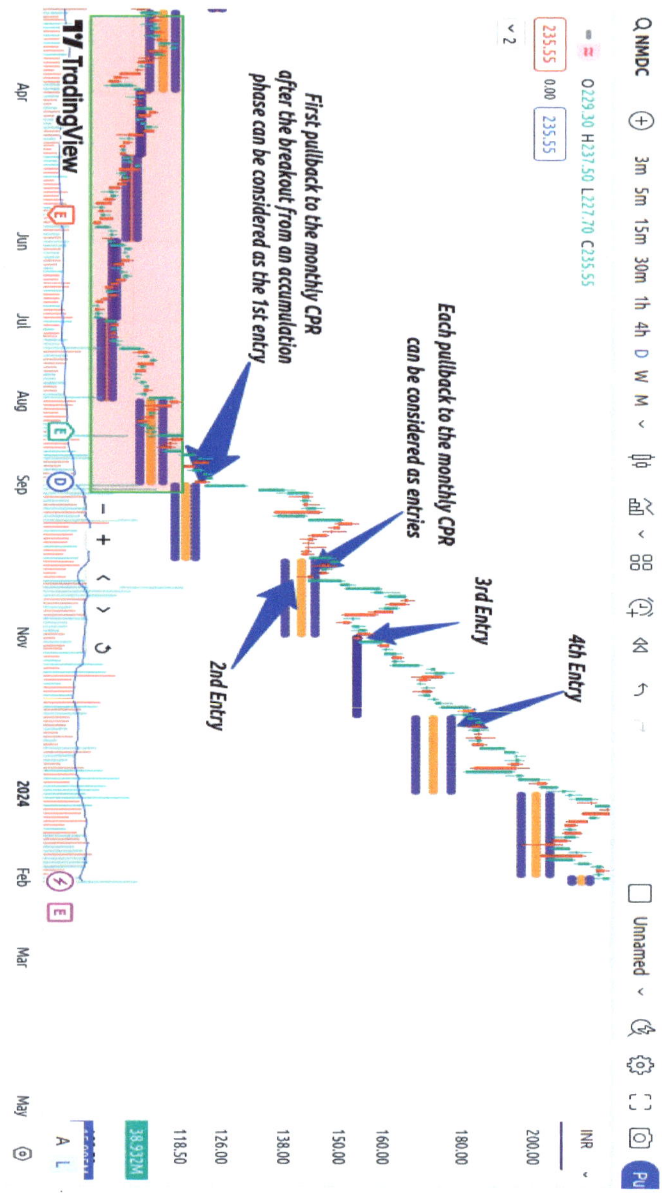
NMDC
O229.30 H237.50 L227.70 C235.55
First pullback to the monthly CPR after the breakout from an accumulation phase can be considered as the 1st entry
Each pullback to the monthly CPR can be considered as entries
2nd Entry
3rd Entry
4th Entry
TradingView
Apr
Jun
Jul
Aug
Sep
Nov
2024
Feb
Mar
May
200.00
180.00
160.00
150.00
138.00
126.00
118.50

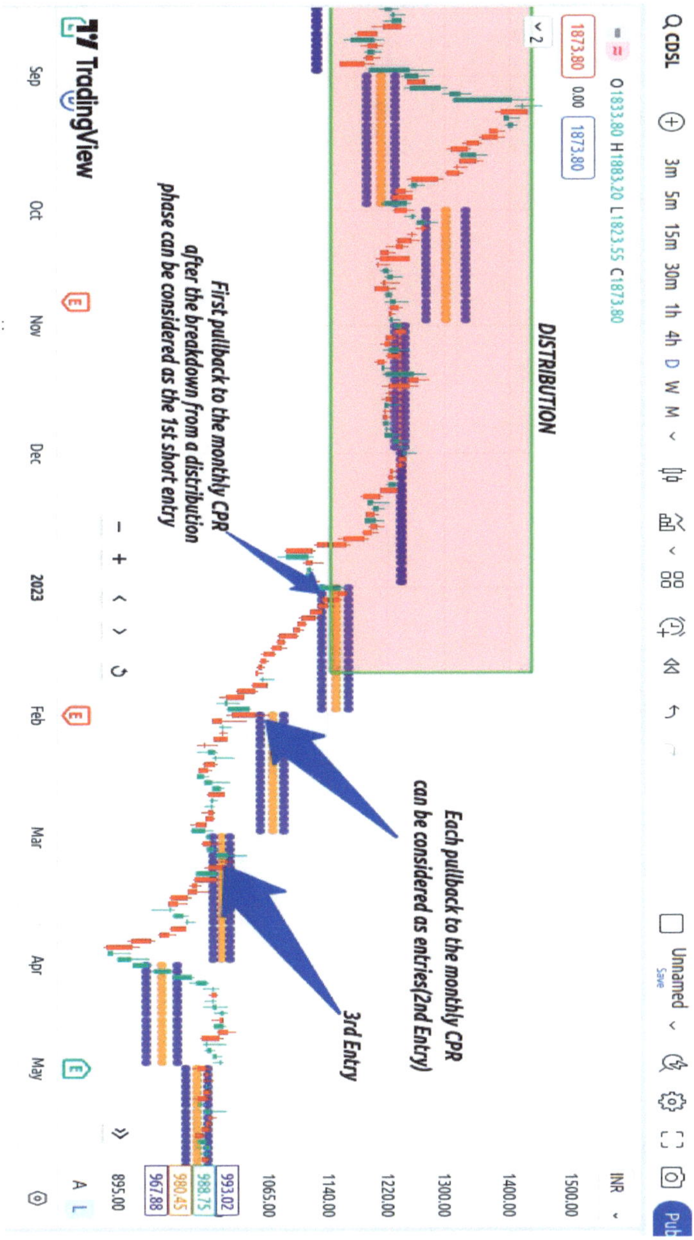
CDSL
O1833.80 H1883.20 L1823.55 C1873.80
DISTRIBUTION
First pullback to the monthly CPR after the breakdown from a distribution phase can be considered as the 1st short entry
Each pullback to the monthly CPR can be considered as entries(2nd Entry)
3rd Entry
TradingView

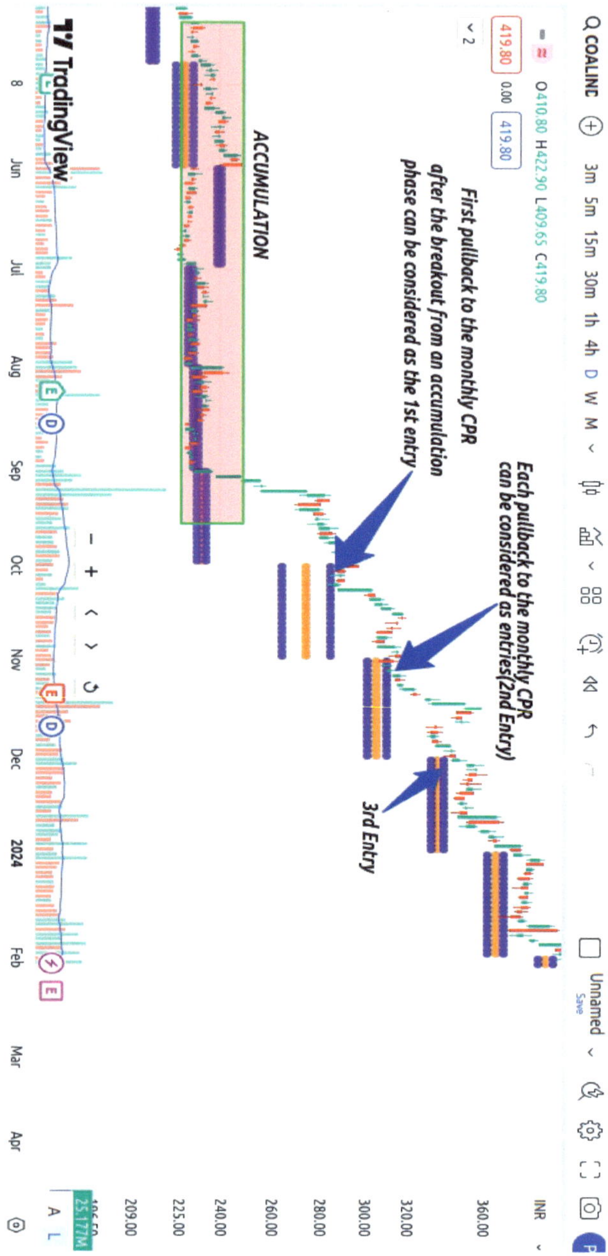
COALINE
O410.80 H422.90 L409.65 C419.80
ACCUMULATION
First pullback to the monthly CPR after the breakout from an accumulation phase can be considered as the 1st entry
Each pullback to the monthly CPR can be considered as entries(2nd Entry)
3rd Entry
TradingView

ACCUMULATION
First pullback to the monthly CPR after the breakout from an accumulation phase can be considered as the 1st entry
Each pullback to the monthly CPR can be considered as entries(2nd Entry)
3rd Entry
TradingView
Mar
Apr
May
Jun
Jul
Aug
Sep
Oct

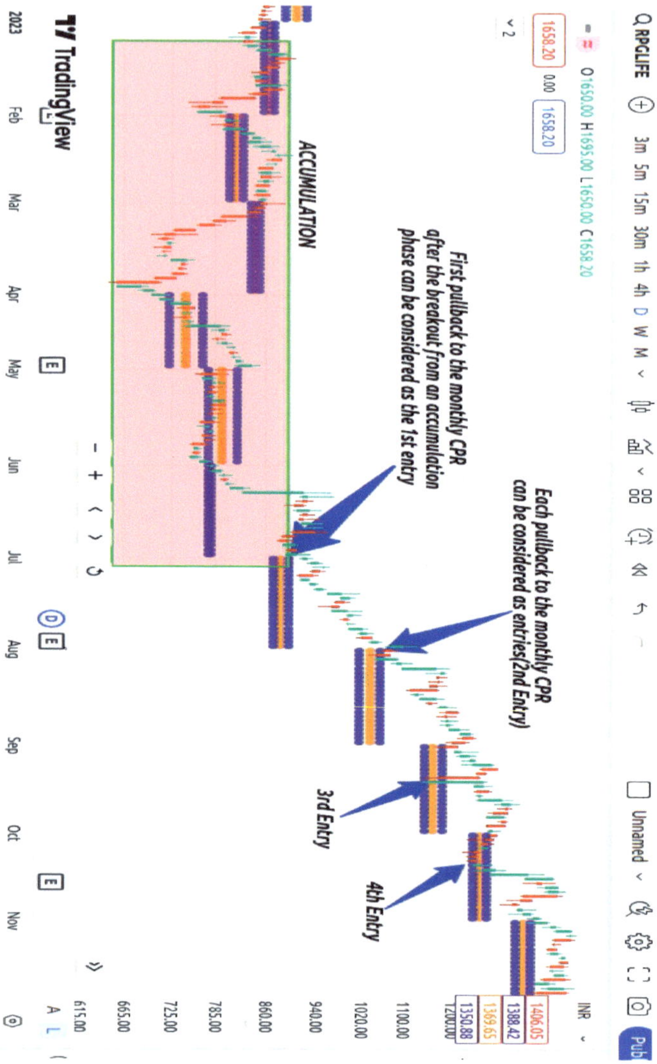
RPGLIFE
O1650.00 H1695.00 L1650.00 C1658.20
1658.20 0.00 1658.20
ACCUMULATION
First pullback to the monthly CPR after the breakout from an accumulation phase can be considered as the 1st entry
Each pullback to the monthly CPR can be considered as entries(2nd Entry)
3rd Entry
4th Entry
TradingView
2023
Feb
Mar
Apr
May
Jun
Jul
Aug
Sep
Oct
Nov
INR
1406.05
1388.42
1369.65
1350.88
1100.00
1020.00
940.00
860.00
785.00
725.00
665.00
615.00

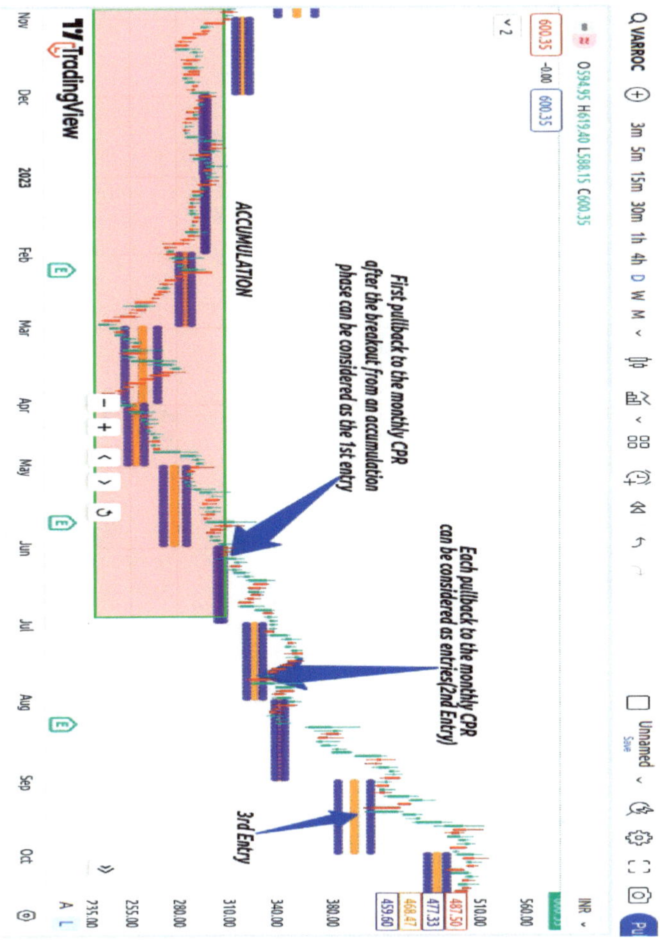
VARROC
ACCUMULATION
First pullback to the monthly CPR after the breakout from an accumulation phase can be considered as the 1st entry
Each pullback to the monthly CPR can be considered as entries(2nd Entry)
3rd Entry
TradingView

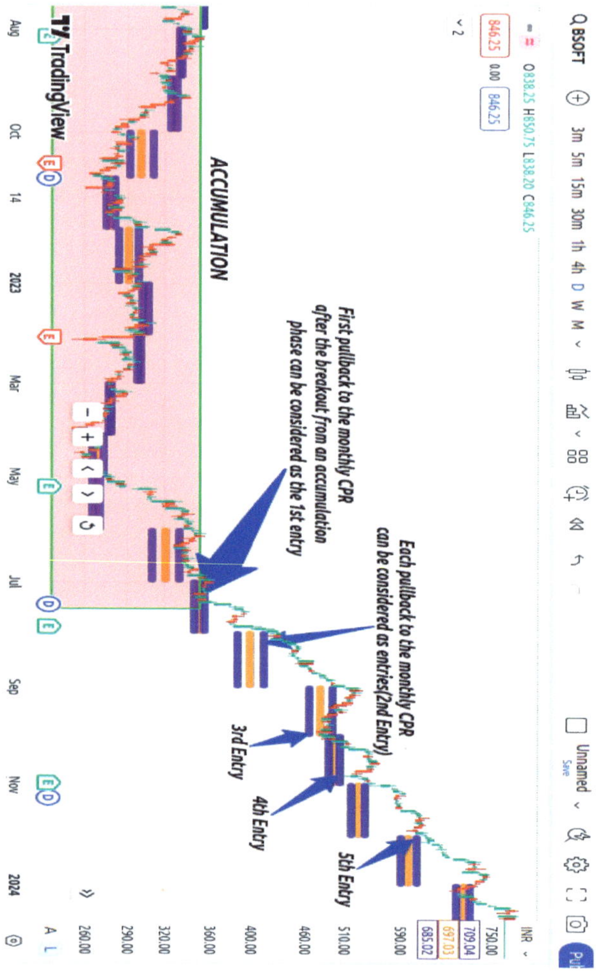
BSOFT
ACCUMULATION
First pullback to the monthly CPR after the breakout from an accumulation phase can be considered as the 1st entry
Each pullback to the monthly CPR can be considered as entries(2nd Entry)
3rd Entry
4th Entry
5th Entry
TradingView

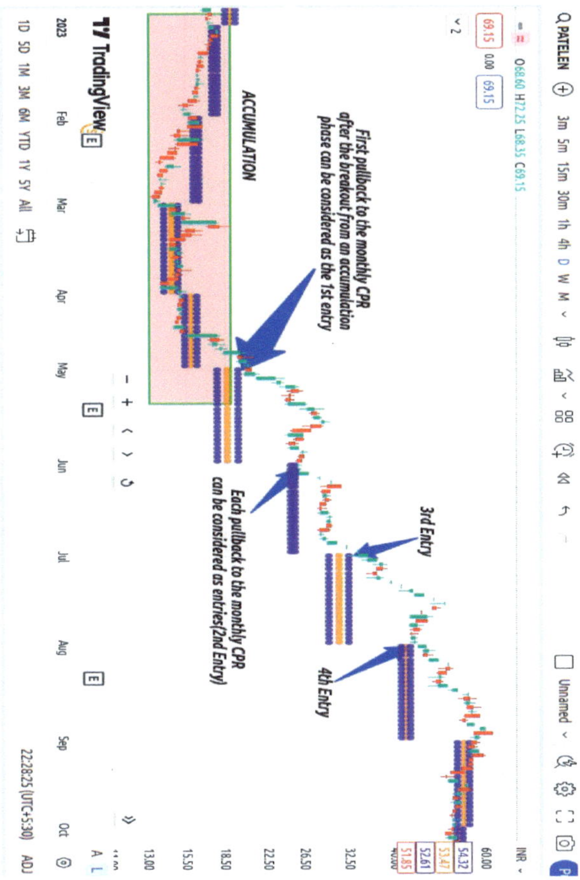
PATELEN
O68.60 H72.25 L68.35 C69.15
ACCUMULATION
First pullback to the monthly CPR after the breakout from an accumulation phase can be considered as the 1st entry
Each pullback to the monthly CPR can be considered as entries(2nd Entry)
3rd Entry
4th Entry
TradingView

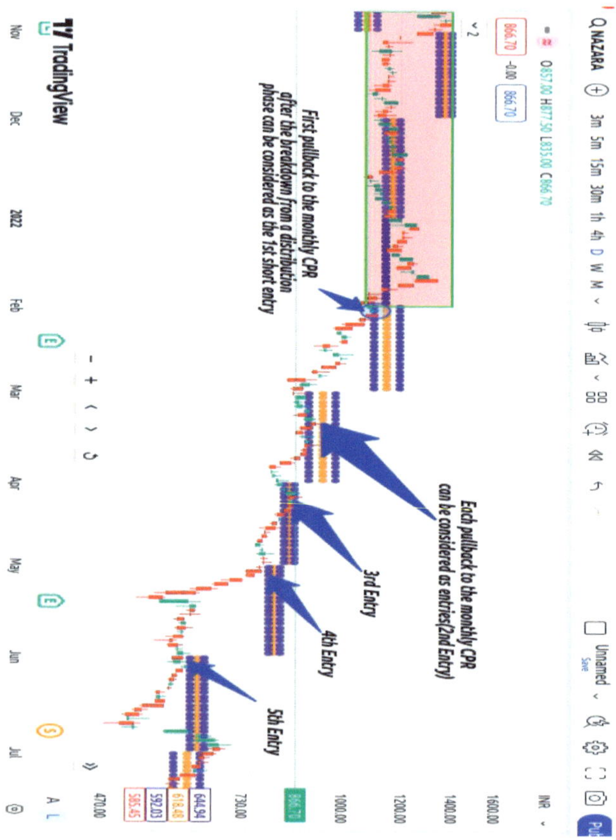
NAZARA
First pullback to the monthly CPR after the breakdown from a distribution phase can be considered as the 1st short entry
Each pullback to the monthly CPR can be considered as entries(2nd Entry)
3rd Entry
4th Entry
5th Entry
TradingView

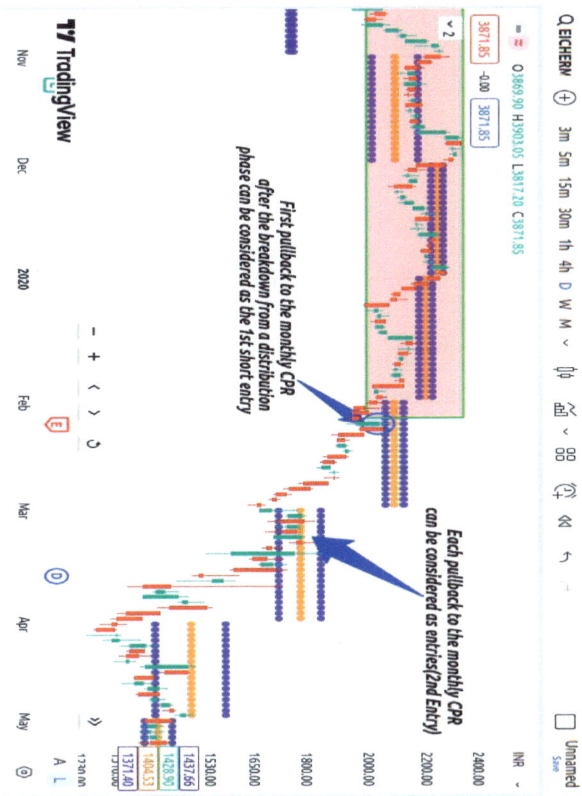
EICHERM
O3869.90 H3903.05 L3817.20 C3871.85
3871.85
-0.00
3871.85
First pullback to the monthly CPR
after the breakdown from a distribution
phase can be considered as the 1st short entry
Each pullback to the monthly CPR
can be considered as entries(2nd Entry)
TradingView
Nov
Dec
2020
Feb
Mar
Apr
May
INR
2400.00
2200.00
2000.00
1800.00
1650.00
1530.00
1437.66
1428.90
1404.53
1371.40

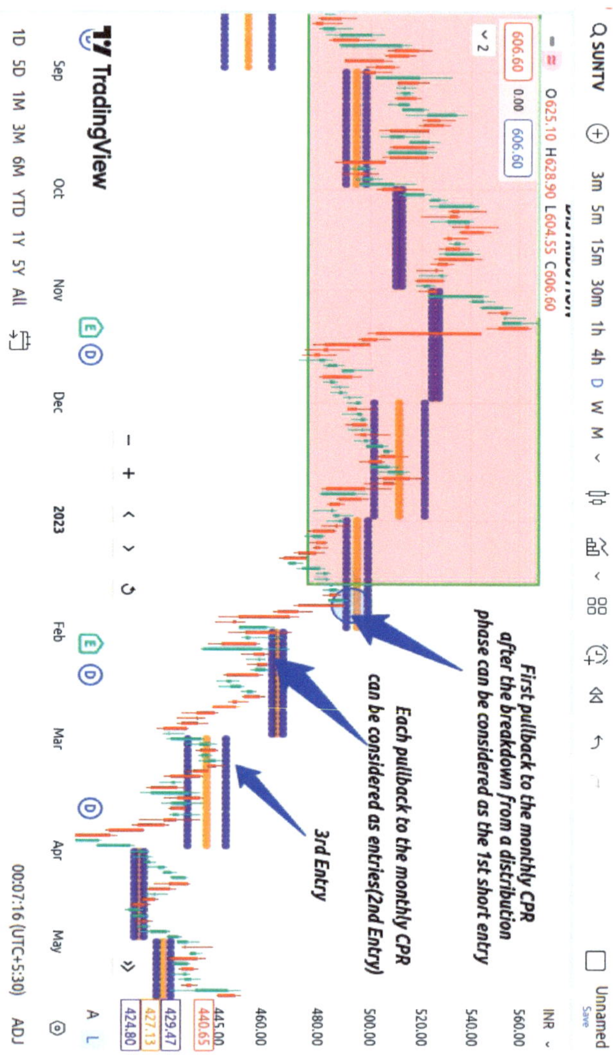
SUNTV
First pullback to the monthly CPR after the breakdown from a distribution phase can be considered as the 1st short entry
Each pullback to the monthly CPR can be considered as entries(2nd Entry)
3rd Entry
TradingView

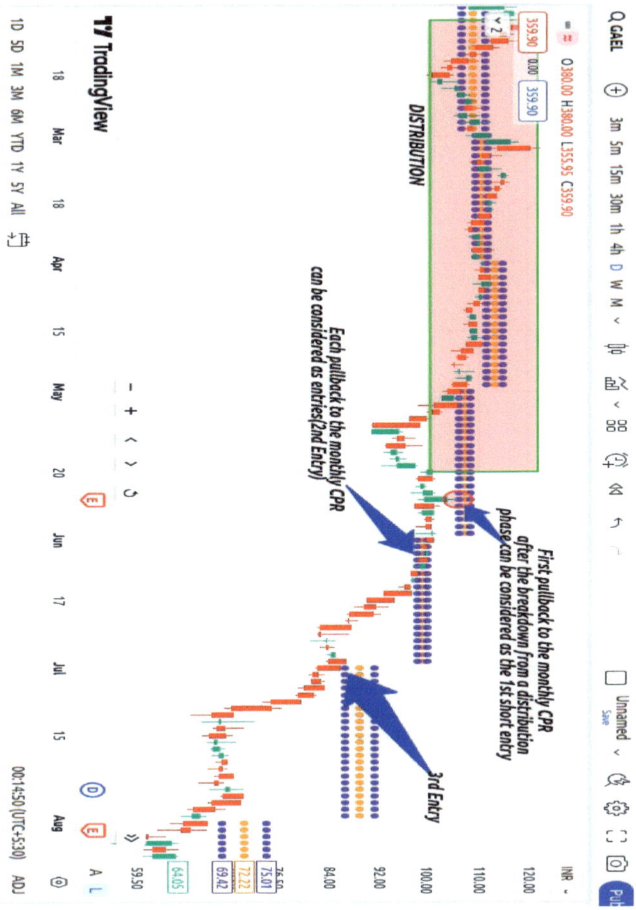
GAEL
O380.00 H380.00 L355.95 C359.90
DISTRIBUTION
First pullback to the monthly CPR after the breakdown from a distribution phase can be considered as the 1st short entry
Each pullback to the monthly CPR can be considered as entries(2nd Entry)
3rd Entry
TradingView

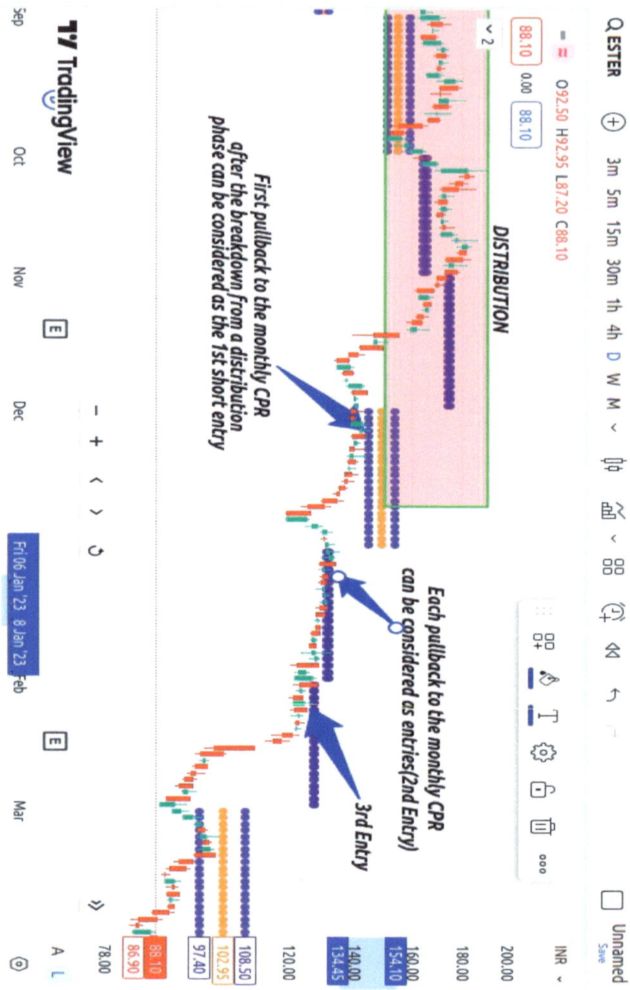
ESTER
O92.50 H92.95 L87.20 C88.10
DISTRIBUTION
First pullback to the monthly CPR after the breakdown from a distribution phase can be considered as the 1st short entry
Each pullback to the monthly CPR can be considered as entries(2nd Entry)
3rd Entry
TradingView

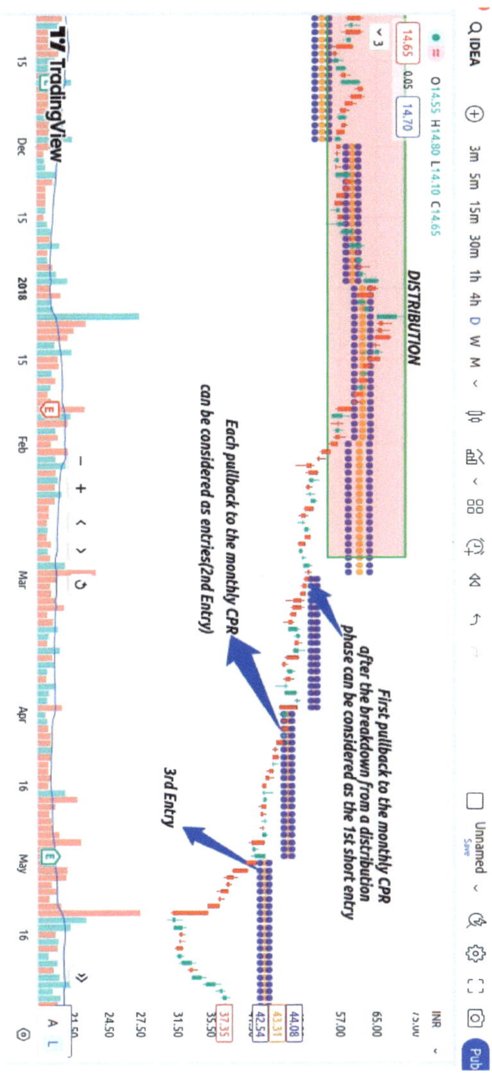
DISTRIBUTION
First pullback to the monthly CPR after the breakdown from a distribution phase can be considered as the 1st short entry
Each pullback to the monthly CPR can be considered as entries(2nd Entry)
3rd Entry

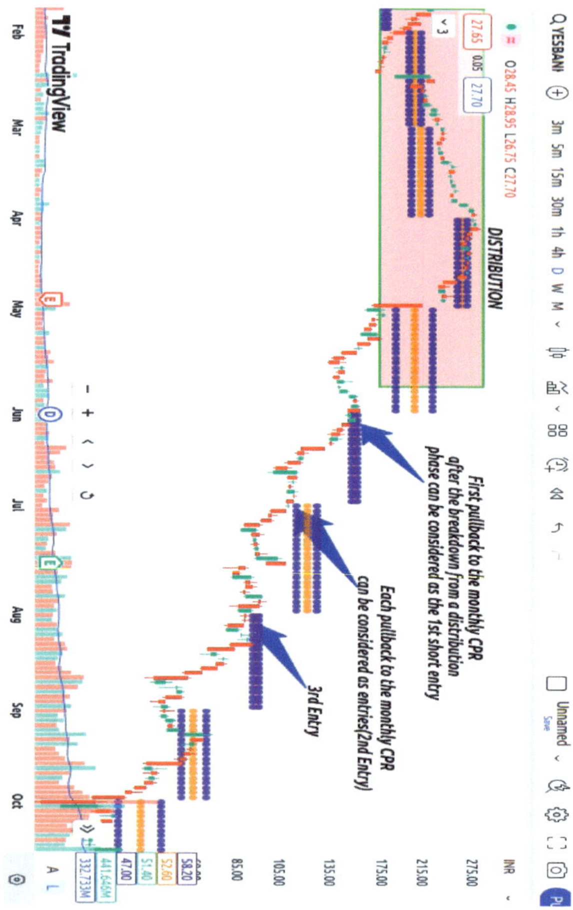

DISTRIBUTION
First pullback to the monthly CPR after the breakdown from a distribution phase can be considered as the 1st short entry
Each pullback to the monthly CPR can be considered as entries(2nd Entry)
3rd Entry
TradingView
Feb
Mar
Apr
May
Jun
Jul
Aug
Sep
Oct

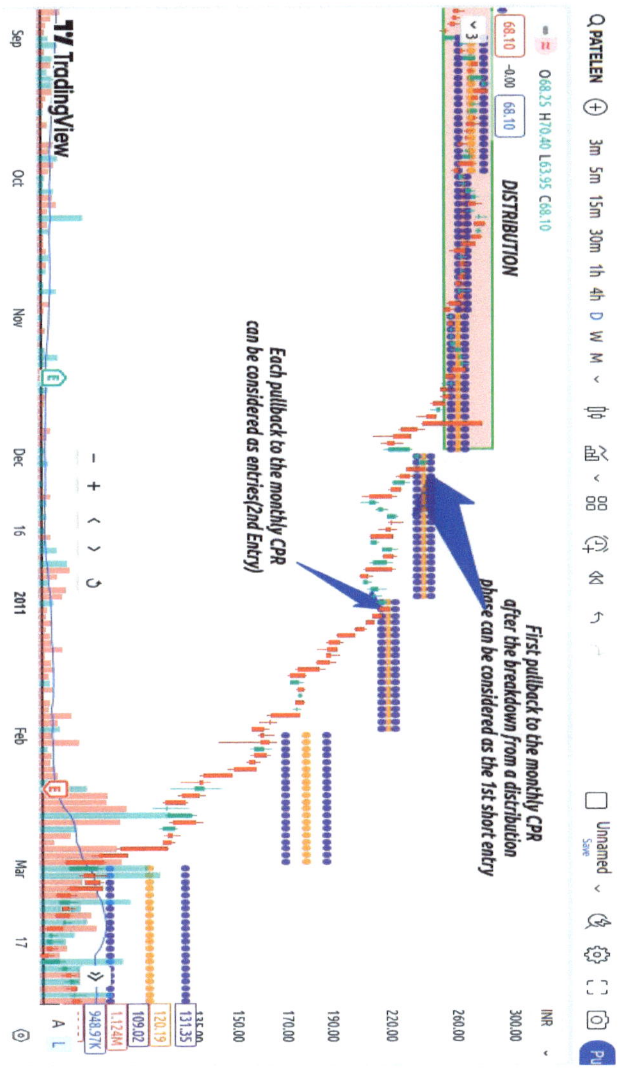
PATELEN
O68.25 H70.40 L63.95 C68.10
DISTRIBUTION
First pullback to the monthly CPR after the breakdown from a distribution phase can be considered as the 1st short entry
Each pullback to the monthly CPR can be considered as entries(2nd Entry)
TradingView
Sep
Oct
Nov
Dec
16
2011
Feb
Mar
17
300.00
260.00
220.00
190.00
170.00
150.00
131.35
120.19
109.02
1.124M
948.97K

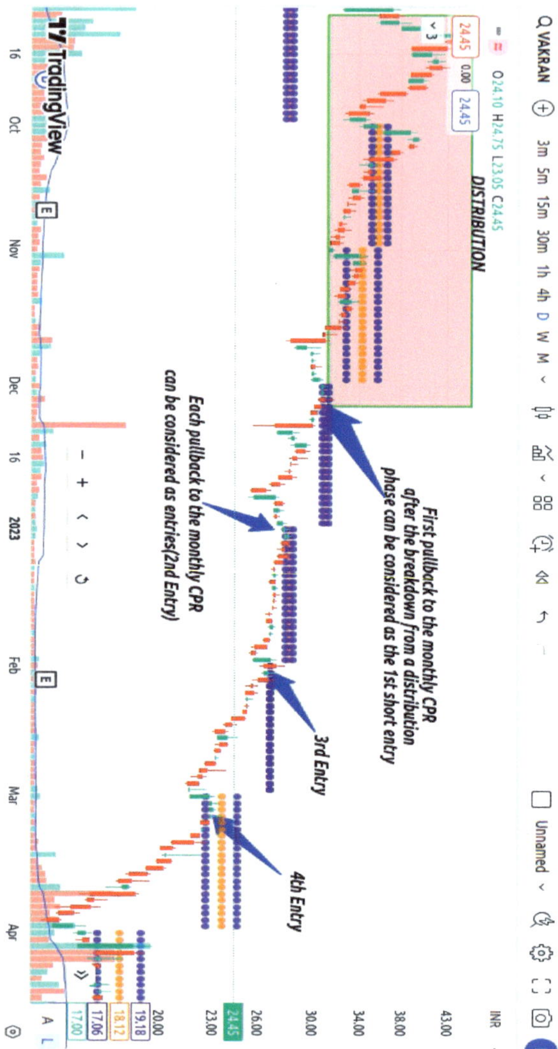
VAKRAN
DISTRIBUTION
First pullback to the monthly CPR after the breakdown from a distribution phase can be considered as the 1st short entry
Each pullback to the monthly CPR can be considered as entries(2nd Entry)
3rd Entry
4th Entry
TradingView

STRATEGY-4

IPO BASED HIGH BREAKOUT STRATEGY

Ever felt like investing in IPOs is a gamble? It often feels like a lottery, doesn't it? But don't worry – there's a way to turn the odds in your favor and potentially earn even better returns than the initial listing gains. Let's explore the IPO-based high breakout strategy and how it can work wonders for your investments.

Understanding the Strategy:

The IPO-based high breakout strategy is all about seizing the opportunity when newly listed stocks start gaining traction. Whether an IPO shoots up or takes a dip, our focus is on marking its highest point. Then, we wait for the stock to break past that point and set alerts to keep us in the loop.

Key Steps:

• **Mark the IPO High**: After an IPO hits the market, note down its highest price, regardless of whether it happens right away or over time.

• **Set Alerts**: Keep tabs on the stock's movement and set alerts for when it breaks above the IPO high.

• **Time to Act**: When the breakout occurs, watch the stock closely. If the day's candle closes above the IPO high, consider making a move.

• **Hold on Tight**: After entering the trade, brace yourself for potential big moves. Based on backtested results and experience, gains of 25% or more could be within reach in just a matter of days or weeks. Partial booking after 20% profit is good in this strategy.

Rationale and Expected Outcomes:

Why does this strategy work? Research suggests that buyers are often drawn to freshly listed stocks, and many stocks tend to hit their peak within the first ten years. So, even if you missed out on the IPO, there's still a chance to jump in when the timing is right.

Comparative Advantage:

Compared to other breakout strategies like multi-year or all-time high breakouts, the IPO-based high breakout strategy stands out for its potential to deliver high profits. Freshly listed stocks often attract significant attention and can experience rapid price movements, making them attractive targets for savvy traders.

Case Studies:

To illustrate the effectiveness of this strategy, we'll dive into real-life examples with detailed chart analysis. These case studies will show how the IPO-based high breakout strategy has delivered impressive returns in the past, giving you the tools to apply it effectively in your own trading journey.

Conclusion:

In the world of swing trading, the IPO-based high breakout strategy offers a straightforward way to capitalize on the momentum of newly listed stocks. By following a systematic approach and leveraging the unique dynamics of IPOs, traders can potentially unlock significant gains within a relatively short time frame.

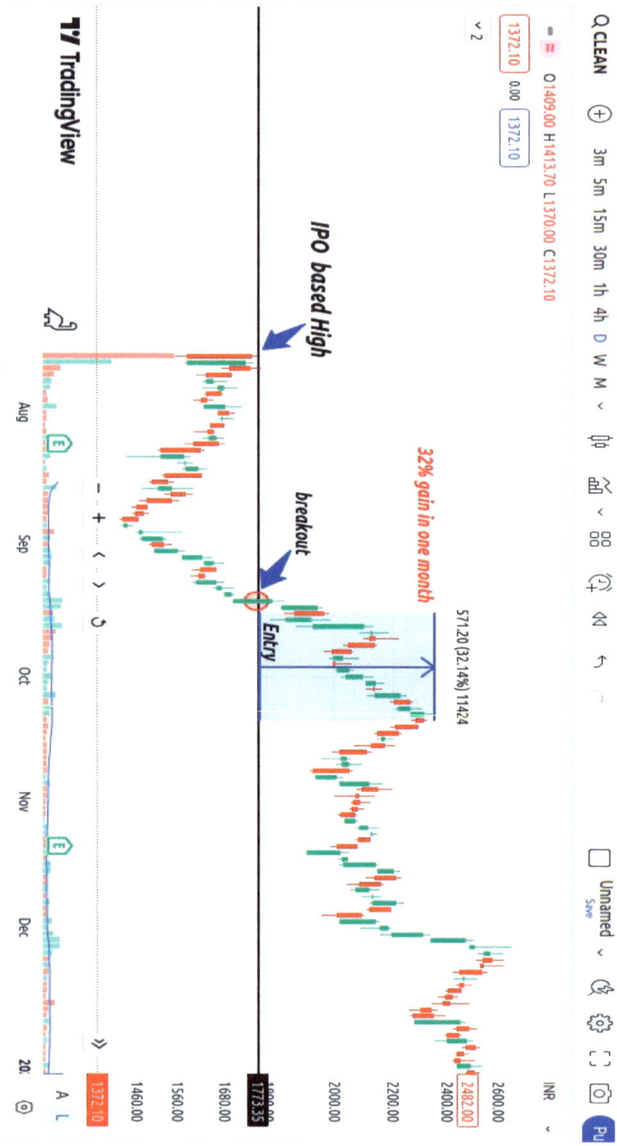
CLEAN
O1409.00 H1413.70 L1370.00 C1372.10
IPO based High
breakout
32% gain in one month
571.20 (32.14%) 11424
Entry
Aug
Sep
Oct
Nov
Dec
TradingView

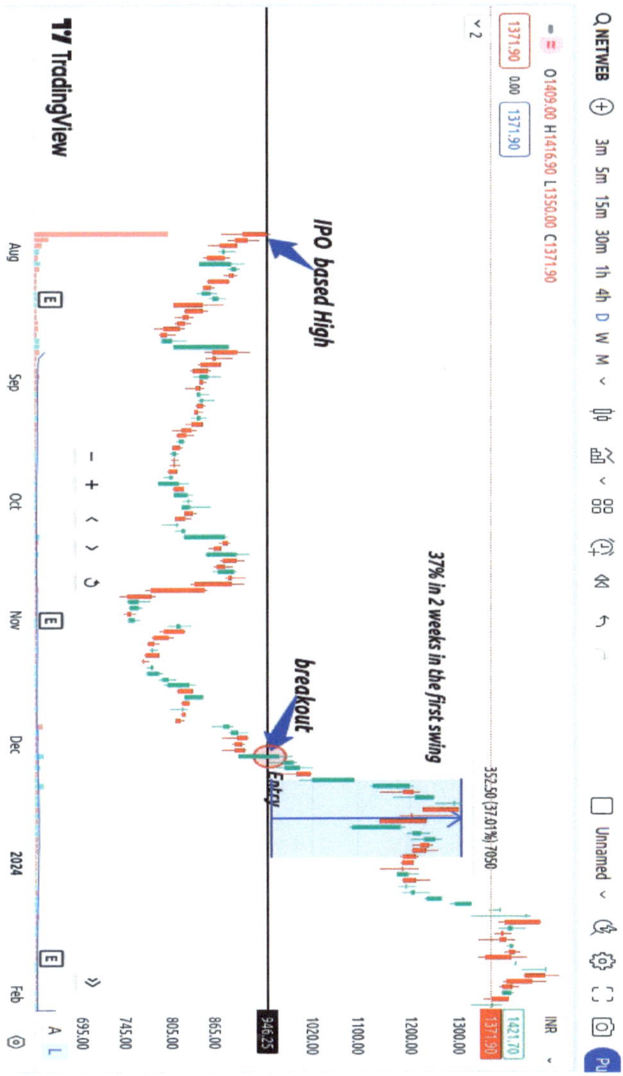
NETWEB
O1409.00 H1416.90 L1350.00 C1371.90
IPO based High
breakout
Entry
37% in 2 weeks in the first swing
352.50 (37.01%) 7050
TradingView

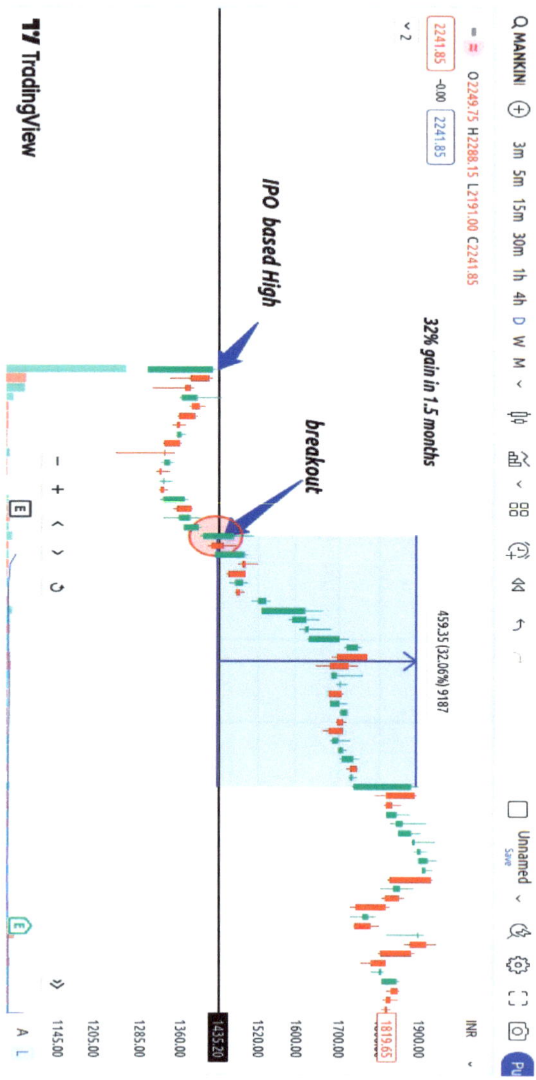
MANKINI
3m 5m 15m 30m 1h 4h D W M
O2249.75 H2288.15 L2191.00 C2241.85
2241.85 -0.00 2241.85
32% gain in 1.5 months
459.35 (32.06%) 9187
IPO based High
breakout
Unnamed
INR
1900.00
1819.65
1700.00
1600.00
1520.00
1435.20
1360.00
1285.00
1205.00
1145.00
TradingView

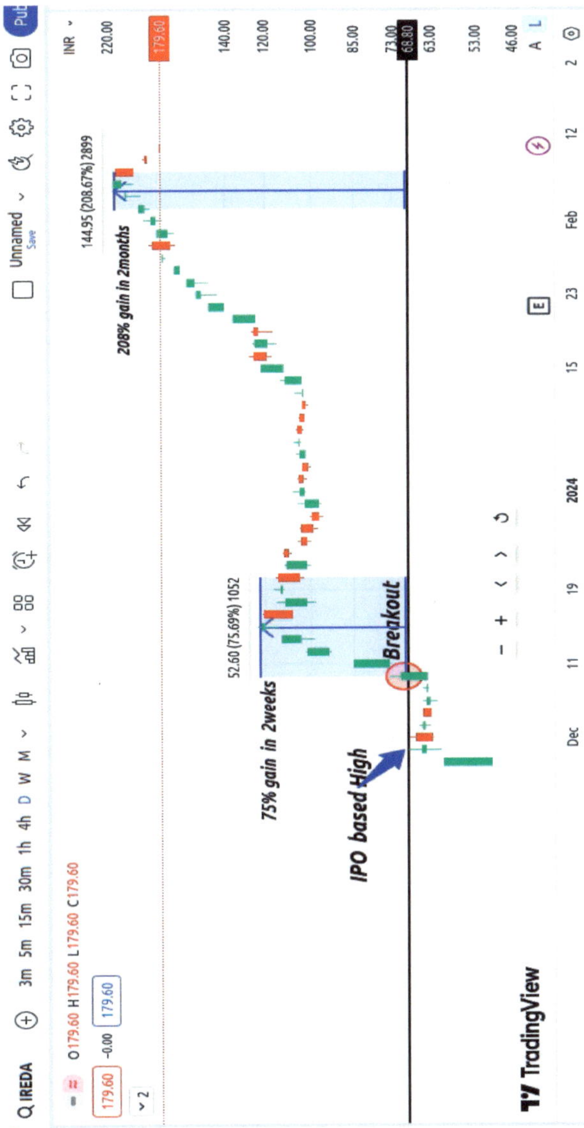
IREDA
O179.60 H179.60 L179.60 C179.60
208% gain in 2months
144.95 (208.67%) 2899
75% gain in 2weeks
52.60 (75.69%) 1052
Breakout
IPO based High
TradingView

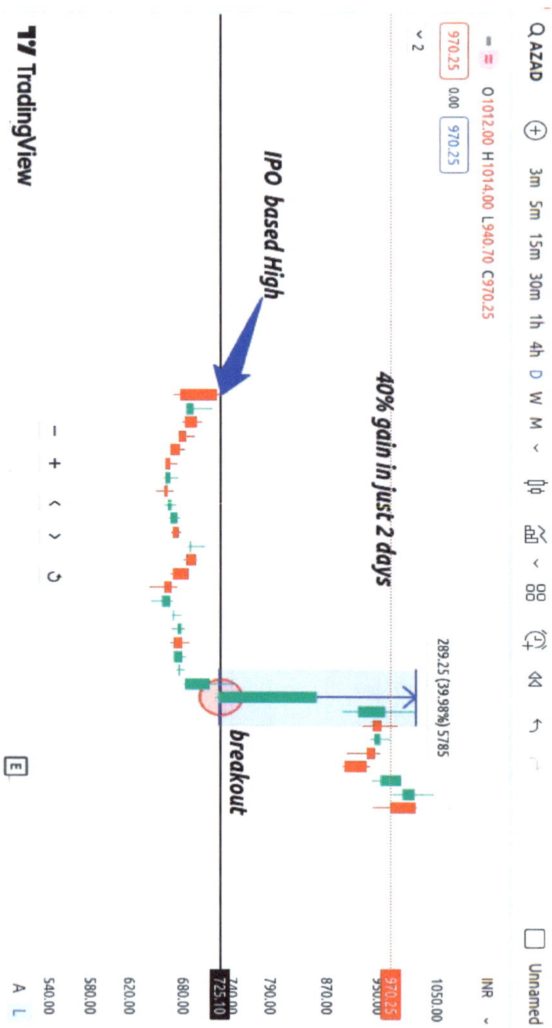
AZAD
O1012.00 H1014.00 L940.70 C970.25
970.25 0.00 970.25
40% gain in just 2 days
289.25 (39.98%) 5785
IPO based High
breakout
TradingView

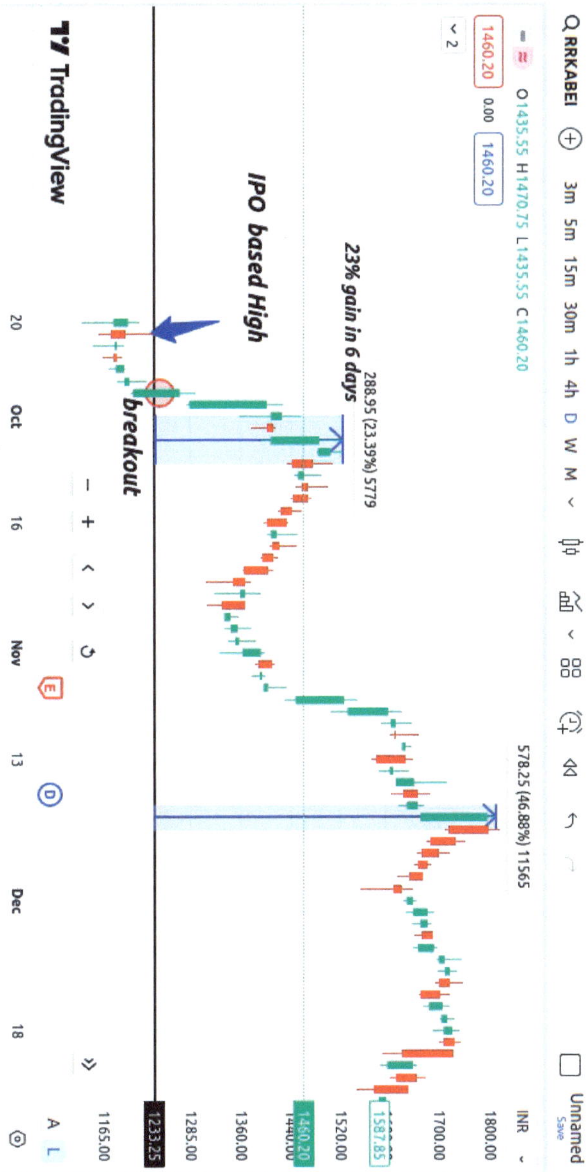
RRKABEI
O1435.55 H1470.75 L1435.55 C1460.20
23% gain in 6 days
288.95 (23.39%) 5779
IPO based High
breakout
578.25 (46.88%) 11565
TradingView

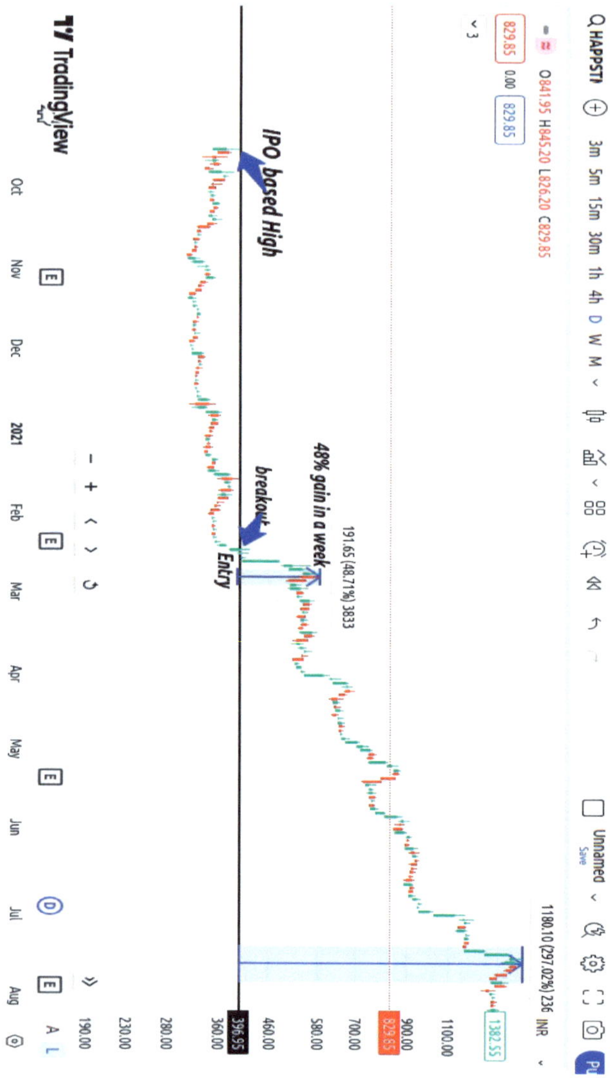
HAPPSTM
O841.95 H845.20 L826.20 C829.85
IPO based High
48% gain in a week
191.65 (48.71%) 3833
breakout
Entry
1180.10 (297.02%) 236
TradingView

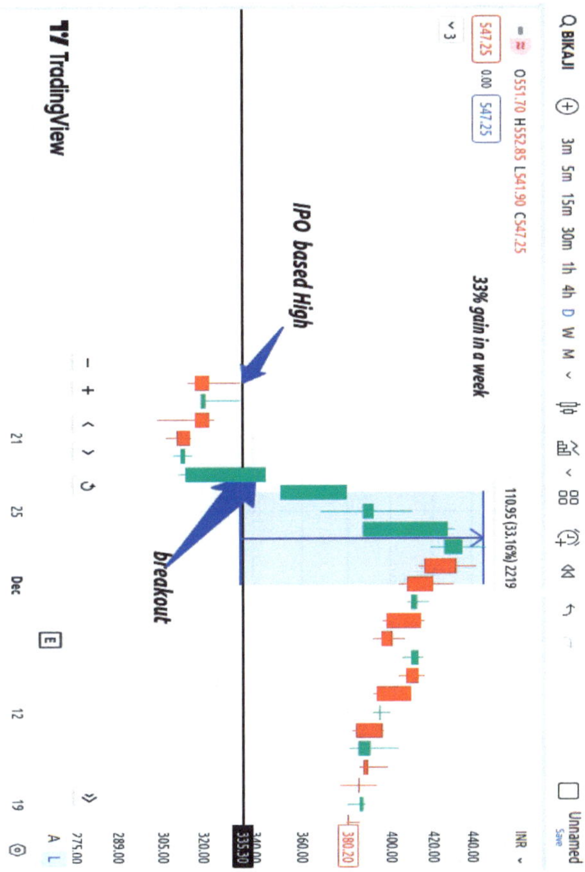
BIKAJI
O551.70 H552.85 L541.90 C547.25
33% gain in a week
110.95 (33.16%) 2219
IPO based High
breakout
TradingView

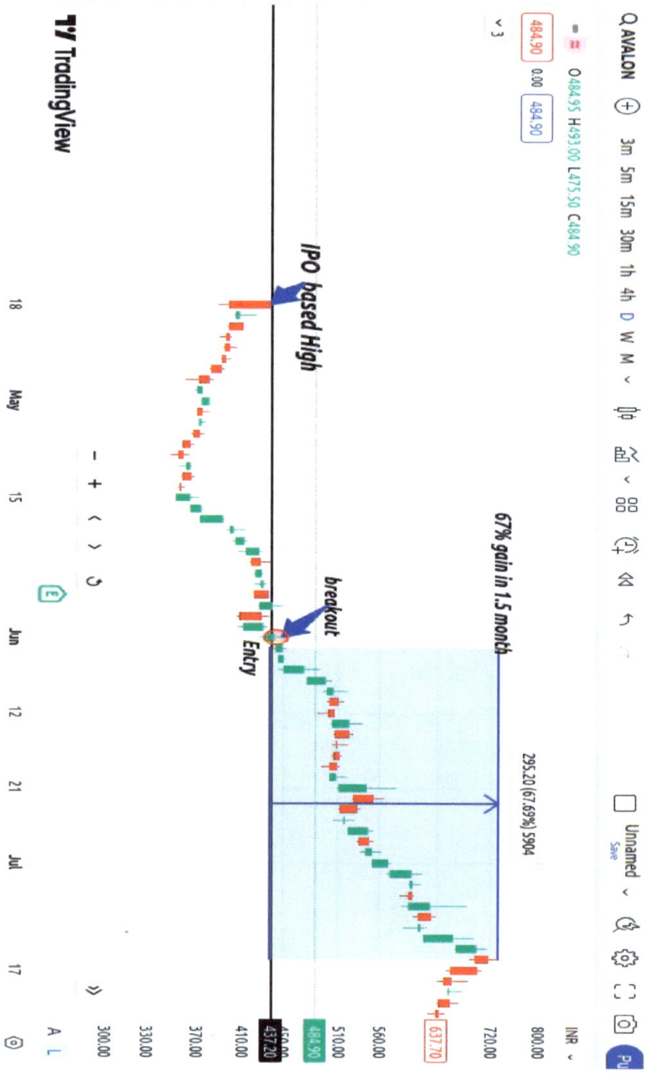
AVALON
O484.95 H493.00 L475.50 C484.90
67% gain in 1.5 month
295.20 (67.69%) 5904
IPO based High
breakout
Entry
TradingView

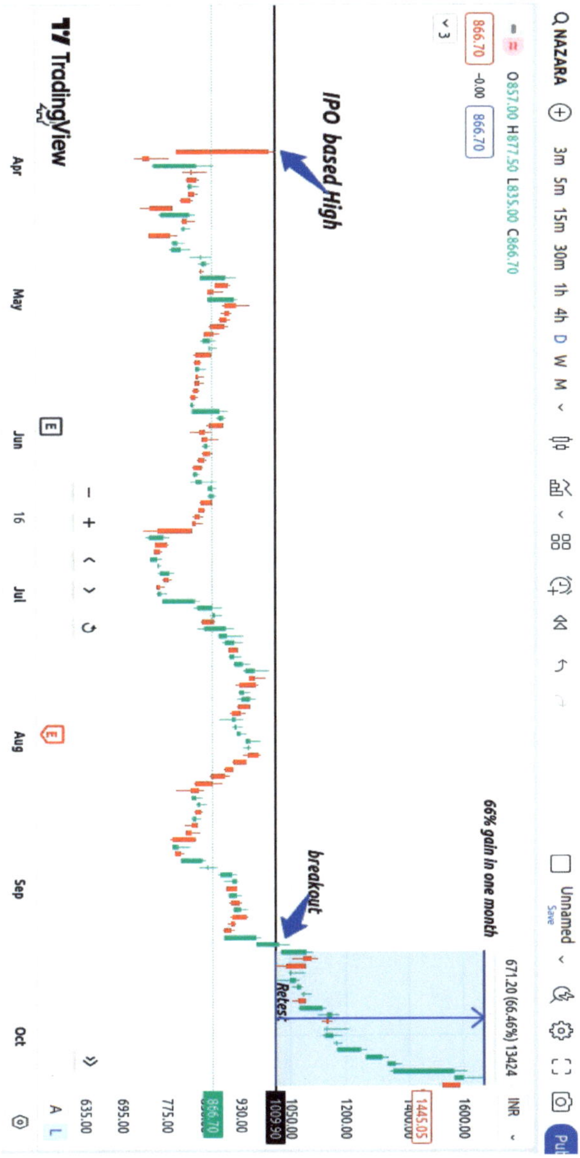
NAZARA
O857.00 H877.50 L835.00 C866.70
866.70
IPO based High
breakout
Retest
66% gain in one month
671.20 (66.46%) 13424
TradingView
Apr
May
Jun
Jul
Aug
Sep
Oct
1600.00
1445.05
1200.00
1050.00
1009.90
930.00
866.70
775.00
695.00
635.00

PART 3

RISK MANAGEMENT, POSITION SIZING AND TRADING PSYCHOLOGY

RISK MANAGEMENT & POSITION SIZING ARE SUPREME

Managing risk is super important. It's crucial to apply effective risk management methods. Decide how much risk you're okay with for each trade. Set stop-loss levels that make sense. Give precedence to risk management over chasing profit targets. When you handle risk well, you keep your money safe and stay in the market for a long time.

- Risk management is the key to successful trading.
- One can be profitable even with a winning rate of 50% or 40% by keeping a Risk reward ratio of 1:2 or 1:3
- You might be wondering how it's possible to be profitable with a coin-tossing probability of 50%.
- That is the wonder of risk management.
- Have minimum 1:2 Risk To Reward in each trade you take (1:2 is minimum, higher the risk reward ratio better it is)

POSITION SIZING

Position sizing refers to the process of determining the amount of capital to invest in a particular trade or investment. In other words Position sizing provides guidance on the number of shares or lots you should purchase or sell .

Effective position sizing is essential for survival in trading.

Position sizing involves following steps

- Calculate your capital
- Decide your Risk per trade (maximum loss you are ready to afford)
    - Maximum you can loss if your SL hits
    - Should not be more than 1-2% of your capital(1% for beginners, 2% for experiences traders)

Position Sizing for each Trade

<u>% Risk per Trade x Capital</u>

Risk per Trade(SL)

- If your capital is 2 lakh ,and you want to buy a stock whose price is 100. As per your strategy the stop loss is 95. Then how many shares should you buy?

- Here Entry price =100
- Stop loss = 95
- Risk per share= 5
- Total Risk taken in this Trade (1%) = 2000
- How many shares can you buy?

<u>% Risk per Trade x Capital</u>

Risk per Trade(SL)

<u>1% x 2,00,000</u> <u>2000</u> = 400 shares

5 5

Position in the stock = 40,000

Profit you can set as at least double of the risk you taken, then you can book profit at 110, then profit will be 4000

Another example

If your capital is 5 lakh ,and you want to buy a stock whose price is 1000. As per your strategy the stop loss is 950. Then how many shares should you buy?

Here Entry price =1000

Stop loss = 950

Risk per share= 50

Total Risk taken in this Trade (1%) = 5000

How many shares can you buy?

$$\frac{\textbf{\% Risk per Trade x Capital}}{\textbf{Risk per Trade(SL)}}$$

$$\frac{1\% \times 5{,}00{,}000}{50} \quad \frac{5000}{50} \quad = 100 \text{ shares}$$

Position in the stock = 1,00,000

Profit you can set as at least double of the risk you taken, then you can book profit at 1100, then profit will be 10,000

Return on 50% Win Rate

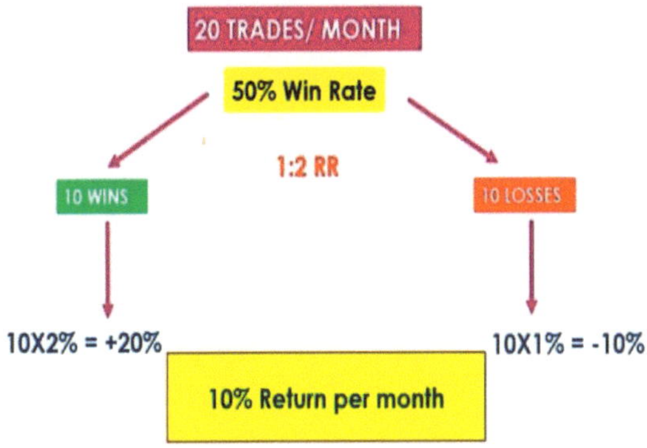

Return on 40% Win Rate

Importance of Position Sizing

Percent Loss of Position	Percent Gain Needed to Get Back to Even
-5%	5.3%
-10%	11.1%
-15%	17.6%
-20%	25.0%
-25%	33.3%
-30%	42.9%
-35%	53.8%
-40%	66.7%
-45%	81.8%
-50%	100.0%
-55%	122.0%
-60%	150.0%
-65%	186.0%
-70%	233.0%
-75%	300.0%
-80%	400.0%
-85%	567.0%
-90%	900.0%

MASTERING TRADING PSYCHOLOGY: ESSENTIAL RULES FOR SUCCESS

1. Unlocking your mindset is key. Your thoughts and beliefs about trading shape your success. Realize the strength of your mind and focus on fostering a positive, disciplined mindset.
2. Trade smart: Craft a solid trading plan with clear entry points, calculated risk, defined exit strategies, and achievable targets, drawing from the strategies outlined in this book. Stick to this plan steadfastly, avoiding impulsive decisions influenced by emotions or external factors. Sticking to your plan fosters discipline and enhances your chances of success.
3. Keep your emotions in check—feelings can cloud your judgment and prompt irrational choices. Master the art of recognizing and managing your emotions effectively. Maintain emotional equilibrium whether you're on a winning streak or navigating a rough patch.
4. Learn to embrace losses—they're just part of the trading game. Treat them as stepping stones for growth. Instead of dwelling on them, use them to fuel your future successes.
5. Keep a trading journal - it's like your personal trading storybook. Write down when you bought and sold, why you made those moves, and how you felt during each trade. Regularly review your journal to identify

what you're doing well and where you can improve in your trading approach.

6. Consistency unlocks success. - Trading success is like running a marathon, not a sprint. Stick to your plan consistently for long-term profitability. Avoid chasing quick gains and focus on building a strong foundation for lasting success.

Dear Traders,

"The Journey Continues

The journey to earning steady profits through trading begins by applying the concepts I've shared in this book regarding strategies, risk management, and trading psychology.
If you have enjoyed this book, PLEASE leave a kind review from where you purchased it. As an independent author, a word of mouth is my only advertising,

No book is perfect. If you notice any errors, omissions, or have any questions about the indicators mentioned in this book, please reach out to me via email at or WhatsApp at 7907919024.

I promise a quick and personal response.

Trading is a challenging and skillful profession. Don't be scared to make mistakes, learn from your mistakes, and keep asking questions. That includes going back to the ideas in this book as you get more experienced!

A Personal Message

Thank you, reader, for coming with me on this journey of understanding price action and trading psychology.

Moving forward and getting better!"

www.ingramcontent.com/pod-product-compliance
Lightning Source LLC
LaVergne TN
LVHW051135210926
848482LV00006B/323
* 9 7 9 8 8 9 4 1 5 5 1 6 6 *